rose
elliot's
vegetarian
meals in
minutes

rose elliot's vegetarian meals in minutes

Collins

This edition published 2005 by Collins
an imprint of HarperCollins*Publishers*
77–85 Fulham Palace Road, London W6 8JB

www.**collins**.co.uk

First published in paperback 1998; previously published
in 1994 as *Rose Elliot's Vegetarian Fast Food.*

Editor: Jane Middleton
Text designer: Joan Curtis
Photographer: Dave Armstrong
Home Economist: Lyn Rutherford
Stylist: Róisín Nield
Illustrator: Lucinda Rogers
Indexer: Susan Bosanko

Cover design: Sarah Christie
Cover photograph © photolibrary.com

For HarperCollins*Publishers*
Publishing Director: Denise Bates
Senior Managing Editor: Angela Newton
Editorial Assistant: Lisa John

A catalogue record for this book is
available from the British Library.

ISBN-13 978 000 719319 6
ISBN-10 0 00 719319 X

Colour reproduction by Amilcare Pizzi, S.p.A
Printed in Singapore by Imago

With book sales of three million, Rose Elliot is Britain's bestselling vegetarian cookery author. She has earned the praise of vegetarians and non-vegetarians alike for the originality and imaginativeness of her recipes.

Her first book, *Simply Delicious*, was written in response to the many requests for recipes she received from visitors to the retreat centre run by her parents, where she then cooked. The book was widely praised and, since then, Rose has written many bestsellers. *Vegetarian Christmas*, *Vegan Feasts*, *The Bean Book* and *Low Fat, Low Sugar* are published in paperback by Thorsons.

Rose Elliot frequently contributes to national magazines, gives cookery demonstrations and broadcasts on radio and television. She lives with her husband, Robert, in Hampshire. Rose has always had a great interest in astrology and has practised this alongside her career as a cookery writer. With Robert she runs a computer-based astrological service which provides high quality personality profiles, forecasts and compatability charts. More details can be obtained from: Rose Elliot Horoscopes, PO Box 16, Eastleigh, Hampshire SO50 5YP.

CONTENTS

PULSES, GRAINS & NUTS

PULSES, GRAINS & NUTS

These are packed full of nutrients. Nuts are a very concentrated source of energy, and small quantities go a long way. They make a wonderful fast food - great for putting into lunchboxes with some salad or fruit for a nourishing, fastest-ever meal. Most pulses need soaking and long cooking, so all the recipes in this book rely on canned ones to save time, except for split red lentils which cook quickly without soaking. Grains are invaluable, too, and are much richer in protein, minerals and vitamins than many people realize.

VEGETABLES

VEGETABLES

Vegetables are excellent fast foods and make the basis of hundreds of speedy dishes. Most are quick to cook or can be served raw, and now that you can buy many of them ready washed the preparation time is even quicker. They can be made into wonderful main courses such as Provençal Potatoes, Broccoli with Cashew Sauce or Grilled Mediterranean Vegetables with Mozzarella; comforting soups, including Green Pea and Mint and Creamy Onion; or salads such as Thai Cabbage Salad or Italian Country Salad; vegetables are so versatile that there's plenty of scope for experiment.

FRUIT

FRUIT

If you're looking for something to give you a quick burst of energy, fruit beats sugary convenience foods any day; it's easy to carry, sweet and delicious to eat, and doesn't make you fat or rot your teeth. But fruit isn't just for snacking. It can also be the basis of starters, such as Three-Pear Salad, and light main courses, such as Apricots with Ricotta and Mint or Tarragon Pear with Cream Cheese. And, of course, fruit is perfect for quick nutritious desserts, from light, refreshing Peaches in Wine or Rhubarb and Ginger Compote to more substantial puddings such as Blueberry Crumble.

THE STORECUPBOARD

Most of the recipes in this book are based on a combination of fresh ingredients and ingredients that keep well in a storecuboard, such as pasta, rice and spices. A well-stocked storecupboard saves time; after the initial stocking-up it's just a matter of replenishing it when required. You don't have to shop every day to make quick vegetarian meals: fresh vegetables and dairy produce keep very well in the fridge; herbs in jugs of water or growing in pots in a light place; and bread, if you want some in reserve, in the freezer. These are the ingredients I find most useful to have in stock, and many of the recipes in this book rely on them.

DRY GOODS

I like to keep in several packets of pasta in different shapes and a supply of split red lentils, which cook more quickly than other pulses and don't need soaking. Various types of rice are also indispensable: brown basmati is the only wholegrain rice that cooks in under 30 minutes, and white basmati takes even less time. Bulgur wheat, couscous, instant polenta, chick pea (gram) flour, cornflour and dried breadcrumbs are worth having for occasional use, and flour (both white and wholemeal) and baking powder are storecupboard basics. Wheatmeal and amaretti biscuits keep fairly well and make a good base for various puddings. Dried fruits are useful for both sweet and savoury dishes, as are nuts, seeds, desiccated coconut, coconut milk powder and creamed coconut. Try to keep several types of nuts and seeds in stock, such as walnuts, hazelnuts, cashews, pine nuts, sunflower seeds and sesame seeds. If possible, store nuts in the fridge or freezer to prevent them from going rancid. In any case, buy them in small quantities.

CANNED AND FROZEN FOOD

Certain canned ingredients are invaluable for making fast food – green lentils, chick peas, different types of beans, canned sweetcorn (without added sugar), artichoke hearts and tomatoes in juice. Canned whole tomatoes are usually of better quality than the chopped ones and it's easy to break them up quickly with a spoon once they're in the saucepan. Canned chestnuts and unsweetened chestnut purée come in handy, whether it's to make a hearty winter stew or whip up a luxurious quick pudding. I like the vacuum-packed canned whole chestnuts that are now available. It's also possible to buy frozen peeled chestnuts. Other frozen foods I like to keep in stock are sweetcorn, petit pois and leaf spinach. Sticks of frozen double or whipping cream are useful, too, for when you need just a small quantity.

FLAVOURING INGREDIENTS

Flavouring ingredients are doubly important for fast food, because you need to add interest and intensity of taste without a lengthy cooking period. It's worth spending a little time and money, therefore, building up a collection of spices and herbs, sweet and savoury flavourings, and good oils and vinegars. At the most basic level, you need good salt – I like flaky Maldon sea salt which you can crush in your fingers – and a grinder for black peppercorns. Other basics are light olive oil for shallow-frying and a good-quality virgin olive oil for salad dressings. For stir-frying and occasional deep-frying I use groundnut oil because it is the most stable at high temperatures; also dark sesame oil for adding flavour to stir-fries and oriental dishes. Vinegars to keep in stock are red wine vinegar, balsamic vinegar and light, sweet brown rice vinegar, all of which have their own individual character. Tabasco sauce and soy sauce pep up food instantly – choose soy sauce that is naturally matured and contains only soya beans and salt. Then there's mustard, preferably smooth Dijon as well as wholegrain Meaux mustard; good bought mayonnaise such as Hellman's; and jars of capers, black olive pâté (the type made only with black olives and olive oil is best), sun-dried tomatoes, pesto sauce and black olives (my favourites are the Greek Kalamata or the little Niçois olives – all of these are best kept in the fridge.

For sweet flavourings, I use both clear and thick honey and stem ginger preserved in syrup; I also find ginger preserve, a kind of ginger jam, useful. Rose and orange flower waters are versatile flavourings, and perhaps even better are liqueurs such as Cointreau or Amaretto, and eau de vie. My favourite is eau de vie de poire William – horribly expensive but divine in a delicate pear dessert.

The spices I find most useful are cinnamon (in sticks and ground) cloves, cardamom, cayenne, chilli powder, whole and ground coriander, whole and ground cumin, ground turmeric, paprika, dried red chillies, and whole nutmegs for grating when needed. Mustard seeds and curry powder are good for occasional use. As far as herbs are concerned, thyme, sage, rosemary and oregano seem to survive the drying process well, and bay is actually better and more concentrated in flavour when dried. Being able to buy fresh herbs easily has made a huge difference to the fast cook's repertoire, and I find they keep well in their little pots or in jars of water – fresh mint, basil, parsley, dill, coriander, chives, chervil, tarragon and parsley (particularly flat-leaf) will liven up your cooking immensely. Lemon grass, green chillies and fresh ginger root are also widely available now, and are best kept in the fridge.

FRESH PRODUCE
Basic dairy produce such as eggs – always free range – milk, cream and yogurt should, of course, be kept in the fridge, along with soft and hard cheeses, including a block of fresh Parmesan for grating as required. Fresh vegetables such as tomatoes, salad leaves, carrots and cabbage keep well in the fridge, too. Other basic standbys are onions, garlic, potatoes, oranges and lemons, which I keep in a cool, dark cupboard, and bread, which goes into a bread crock, with a back-up supply in the freezer.

EQUIPMENT

The right equipment makes all the difference to the ease with which you can cook fast food. A little time spent removing clutter, re-thinking your needs, and streamlining and reorganizing kitchen surfaces and cupboards can save hours of your time over the weeks and months.

It's essential to invest in efficient kitchen tools. You don't need a lot of fancy equipment: the most important thing is a really good, sharp knife, and for that you do get what you pay for. Personally I like a classic Sabatier knife with a medium-length (11 cm/4½ inch) blade. A good, solid chopping board is essential, too, the bigger the better. The other small tools I find indispensable are a swivel potato peeler with a long handle that is really comfortable to hold, and a citrus zester, which is a curiously useful

gadget. A garlic press is more bother than it is worth, in my opinion – you can do the job much more quickly and effectively with a knife and a board.

A food processor isn't essential, and many of the recipes in this book can be made without one, but it does open up many more possibilities – lovely creamy soups, quick pâtés and dips, for instance. As with so many things, if you're buying one it pays to get a larger version than you think you'll need; go for something simple in design which doesn't try to do too many jobs. Try to make a space for it on your work surface so that it's always there at the ready. An electric hand whisk is also a surprisingly useful and labour-saving piece of equipment, and fairly inexpensive to buy. For years I put off buying one, and when eventually I did I couldn't believe how useful it was and wondered why I hadn't bought one earlier.

A microwave oven isn't essential by any means, and apart from a microwave version of risotto none of the recipes in this book depend on one. I find a pressure cooker more useful than a microwave because I love making soups and it cooks them very quickly. Some people are wary of pressure cookers because of all their hissing, but once you know what you are doing it can be invaluable.

Finally, a large saucepan with a steamer on top is helpful if you're cooking with limited hob space, because you can have one item cooking in the pan and a vegetable or something else steaming in the top. I have a stainless-steel steamer that I use a lot in this way.

BREAD

There's a huge range of delicious breads around now, and it's fun to try different types. In this section I've included some of my favourites – not just breads and rolls but also more unusual products such as poppadums and tortillas, as well as croissants, bagels, panettone and brioche. Plenty of other interesting baked goods are worth experimenting with, and they all make an ideal basis for fast food. For a long time bread was unfairly dismissed as 'stodge', but now it is recognized as a healthy food which contributes valuable minerals and vitamins, as well as protein and energy, to our diet.

CROSTINI & BRUSCHETTA
✳

These Italian toasts are really very similar: crostini are delicate rounds of light, crisp bread whereas bruschetta is made from coarse country bread and rubbed with garlic to flavour it. They can be served plain to accompany soup, salads or dips, or topped with all kinds of delicious things to make canapés, quick snacks or light meals. If you are making a meal of them they are good served with some salad. You can use either a small or large baguette for crostini, depending on how big you want the rounds to be, and since one baguette yields about 50 slices, you only need a small piece to make a snack or meal for two people.

BASIC RECIPE

4 slices from a large baguette or 8 slices from a small one, cut 6 mm / ¼ inch thick, for crostini
2 slices from a country-style loaf for bruschetta

olive oil
1 garlic clove, peeled and cut in half, for bruschetta

1 Lay the slices of bread on a grill pan and grill until they are dried out and slightly golden on one side, then turn them over and grill the second side.
2 For crostini, brush the slices lightly with olive oil if you wish; I prefer them without. For bruschetta, rub the cut clove of garlic lightly over the surface and brush or drizzle with some olive oil. Serve plain, or with any of the toppings suggested below.
SERVES 2

TOPPINGS

All these toppings make enough for 8 small or 4 large crostini, or 2 bruschetta. Serve the crostini or bruschetta as soon as possible after adding the toppings.

— 1 —
CHERRY TOMATOES, FETA AND THYME

6–8 cherry tomatoes
crostini or bruschetta (see above)
50g / 2oz feta cheese

sprigs of thyme
freshly ground black pepper

1 Slice the cherry tomatoes and arrange them over the crostini or bruschetta then crumble the feta cheese over them.
2 Snip a little fresh thyme over that and add a grinding of black pepper.

— 2 —
BLACK OLIVE PATE, RED PEPPER AND CAPERS

1 red pepper
black olive pâté
crostini or bruschetta (see above)

2–3 tsp capers
a few leaves of flat-leaf parsley

1 Cut the pepper into quarters then grill it for about 10 minutes or until the skin has blistered and charred in places.

2 Cool slightly, then remove the skin and seeds and slice or chop the flesh.

3 Spread black olive pâté over the crostini or bruschetta then top with the red pepper, capers and a few leaves of flat-leaf parsley.

— 3 —
AUBERGINE AND MINT

1 medium aubergine	salt and freshly
olive oil	ground black pepper
4 sprigs of mint	crostini or bruschetta
balsamic vinegar	(see page 12)

1 Slice the aubergine into rounds about 3 mm/⅛ inch thick and lay them on the grill pan.

2 Brush with olive oil on both sides then grill on high for 5–10 minutes, until golden brown and tender.

3 Tear the mint sprigs and mix with the aubergine. Add a few drops of balsamic vinegar and salt and pepper to taste then divide between the crostini or bruschetta.

— 4 —
LENTILS WITH CRANBERRIES

This Christmassy variation can be made very quickly with canned lentils.

1 small onion, peeled and chopped	crostini or bruschetta (see page 12)
1 tbls olive oil	2 tbls cranberry sauce, preferably containing whole cranberries
1 × 425g / 15oz can of lentils	sprigs of flat-leaf parsley

1 Fry the onion in the olive oil for 7–10 minutes, until soft and lightly browned.

2 Drain the lentils and add to the onion, mashing them a bit so that they hold together.

3 Spread this mixture on top of the crostini or bruschetta, piling it up well.

4 Dot the cranberry sauce over the top and decorate with sprigs of flat-leaf parsley.

— 5 —
BLUE CHEESE WITH GRAPES, PINE NUTS AND CHICORY

crostini or bruschetta (see page 12)	125g / 4oz blue cheese 6 black grapes
a few leaves of chicory	a few pine nuts

1 Cover the crostini or bruschetta with chicory leaves, breaking or shredding them as necessary.

2 Thinly slice the blue cheese and arrange on top.

3 Halve and pip the grapes and lay these on top, then scatter over a few pine nuts.

— 6 —
GOAT'S CHEESE, ROCKET AND SUN-DRIED TOMATO

125g / 4oz soft white goat's cheese	several rocket leaves freshly ground black
crostini or bruschetta (see page 12)	pepper
8 sun-dried tomatoes in oil, drained	

1 Spread the soft white goat's cheese thickly on the crostini or bruschetta.

2 Chop the sun-dried tomatoes and arrange them on top of the goat's cheese, together with a few leaves of rocket, then grind some black pepper coarsely over the top.

— 7 —
HUMMUS, OLIVE AND PAPRIKA

125g / 4oz hummus	olive oil
crostini or bruschetta (see page 12)	8 black olives a few sprigs of
paprika pepper	flat-leaf parsley

1 Spread the hummus thickly on top of the crostini or bruschetta. Sprinkle some paprika pepper over the top, then drizzle a little olive oil on top of that.

2 Decorate with the black olives and a sprig or two of flat-leaf parsley.

You can buy very good hummus at most of the big supermarkets and it makes an excellent topping for crostini.

— 8 —

MUSHROOM PATE

225g / 8oz mushrooms
25g / 1 oz butter
1 garlic clove, crushed
2 eggs or 4 quail's eggs

salt and freshly
  ground black pepper
crostini or bruschetta
  (see page 12)
black olive pâté

1 Wash and dry the mushrooms then chop them finely (use a food processor for this if you have one). Melt the butter in a saucepan, put in the mushrooms and garlic and cook them over a fairly high heat until the mushrooms are tender and any liquid they produce has evaporated – this may take 10 minutes.
2 Meanwhile, boil the eggs for 10 minutes or the quail's eggs for 2½ minutes. Shell them and slice them fairly thinly, or cut the quail's eggs in half. Season with salt and pepper.
3 Season the mushroom mixture then either leave it to cool slightly or spread it on the crostini or bruschetta while still hot. Top with the egg slices and a little black olive pâté.

— 9 —

PLUM TOMATO, MOZZARELLA AND BASIL

Plum tomatoes usually have a good flavour and nice firm texture, but you could use other well-flavoured tomatoes.

4 fresh plum tomatoes
salt and freshly
  ground black pepper
olive oil
50g / 2oz Mozzarella
  cheese (packed in
  water)

crostini or bruschetta
  (see page 12)
8 fresh basil leaves

1 Slice the tomatoes into rounds, put them on a plate and sprinkle them with salt, pepper and a few drops of olive oil. Cut the Mozzarella cheese into small pieces.
2 Arrange the tomatoes on top of the crostini or bruschetta then dot the cheese over the tomatoes.
3 Tear the basil leaves over the top of the tomatoes and cheese and grind over some more black pepper to taste.

— 10 —

GOLDY GREENY SPREAD

A strange and interesting recipe, adapted from New Food For All Palates *by Sally and Lucian Berg (Gollancz, 1967). Frozen beans are fine for this.*

1 onion, peeled and
  thinly sliced
2 tbls olive oil
125g / 4oz green beans
1 egg, hard-boiled

salt and freshly ground
  black pepper
crostini or bruschetta
  (see page 12)

1 Fry the onion in the oil until golden brown and crisp (this is very important for the flavour).
2 Cook the green beans in a little boiling water for 3–4 minutes, until tender, then drain.
3 Shell and roughly chop the hard-boiled egg. Put the beans, egg and half the onion into a food processor and whizz to a purée. Season to taste.
4 Spread on top of the crostini or bruschetta and top with the remaining onion.

— 11 —

PECORINO AND PEAR ON WATERCRESS

125g / 4oz soft pecorino
  cheese
crostini or bruschetta
  (see page 12)
a little milk (optional)
a few watercress leaves

1 ripe dessert pear
50g / 2oz hard pecorino
  or Parmesan cheese,
  grated
freshly ground black
  pepper

1 Spread the soft pecorino cheese over the crostini or bruschetta (mix the cheese with a little milk first if necessary).
2 Press the watercress into the cheese. Peel, core and thinly slice the pear and arrange on top.
3 Sprinkle generously with the grated cheese and grind some pepper over, then serve straight away or flash under a hot grill to melt the cheese.

OPPOSITE: *A selection of Crostini, topped with* **Mushroom Pâté, Plum Tomato, Mozzarella and Basil,** *and* **Goldy Greeny Spread**

QUICK PIZZAS
---*✴*---

*It's unrealistic to try and make a pizza from scratch in 30 minutes but you can make a
good quick tomato sauce, spread it over a ready-made base, add a topping
and flash it under a hot grill. Although you can buy pizza bases, I like to use a range of different
breads, such as granary, ciabatta and muffins. The bases and toppings in the following recipes
can be mixed and matched, if you prefer, to suit whatever ingredients you have to hand.*

TOMATO SAUCE

1 tbls olive oil
1 onion, peeled and
  chopped
2 garlic cloves, crushed
1 × 400g / 14oz can
  tomatoes

8 sun-dried tomatoes
  in oil, drained
  (optional)
salt and freshly
  ground black pepper

To make a quick lettuce salad, cut 1 or 2 little gem lettuces across into thick slices; wash and drain in a colander, then put into a bowl, sprinkle with 1 tablespoon of lemon juice, 2 tablespoons of olive oil, some sea salt and freshly ground black pepper, and toss lightly.

1   Heat the oil in a saucepan, add the onion then cover and cook gently for 10 minutes, until tender but not brown.

2   Stir the garlic into the onion, cook for 1–2 minutes longer, then stir in the tomatoes, together with their juice, breaking them up with a wooden spoon. Chop the sun-dried tomatoes roughly, if you are using them, and add these to the pan too.

3   Let the mixture simmer away for about 10–15 minutes until the liquid has evaporated. Season with salt and pepper to taste.
MAKES ENOUGH FOR 2 MUFFINS, OR 1 GRANARY OR CIABATTA PIZZA

MUSHROOM PIZZA

225g / 8oz button
  mushrooms
2 tbls olive oil
salt and freshly
  ground black pepper
2 muffins

125g / 4oz Cheddar or
  other cheese
tomato sauce (see
  above)

1   Wash and slice the mushrooms then fry them in the olive oil for 1–2 minutes until they are tender. Season with salt and pepper.

2   Cut the muffins in half and toast on both sides under the grill. Thinly slice the cheese.

3   Heat the tomato sauce then spread it over the muffins. Top with the mushrooms and cheese and heat under the grill for a few minutes, until the pizzas are piping hot and the cheese is golden brown and bubbling.
SERVES 2

RED AND YELLOW PEPPER PIZZA

1 red pepper
1 yellow pepper
1 oval or round
  granary loaf
  (400g / 14oz)
olive oil
tomato sauce (see
  above)

salt and freshly
  ground black pepper
50g / 2oz Parmesan
  cheese
a few fresh basil
  leaves

1   Cut the peppers into quarters, put them cut-side down on a grill pan and grill for about 10 minutes or until the skin has blistered and charred in places. Remove from the grill and, when cool enough to handle, peel off the skin, remove the seeds and stem, and slice the peppers.

2   Cut the loaf horizontally in half, scoop out a

little of the crumb, then brush the inside with olive oil and toast it under the grill. Toast both sides if you want a crisp pizza base.

3. Heat the tomato sauce then spread this evenly over the bread and top with the peppers, mixing up the colours. Season the peppers lightly, then grate the cheese and sprinkle it over the pizzas.

4. Heat the pizzas under the grill for a few minutes until they are piping hot and the cheese is melted and lightly browned. Tear a little basil over the top and serve.

SERVES 2–4

CIABATTA PIZZA WITH ARTICHOKES

The nicest artichoke hearts to use for this are the ones that you can buy preserved in oil. Any that are left over keep well in the fridge. Alternatively, drained canned artichoke hearts make a good substitute.

1 red onion, peeled and sliced	**125g / 4oz Mozzarella cheese**
olive oil	**125g / 4oz artichoke hearts, sliced**
1 ciabatta loaf	
tomato sauce (see opposite)	

1. Fry the onion in 1 tablespoon of olive oil until softened, about 5–7 minutes.

2. Meanwhile, cut the loaf horizontally in half, brush each cut surface with olive oil and toast it under the grill. Toast both sides if you want a crisp pizza base.

3. Heat the tomato sauce then spread it evenly over the bread. Slice the cheese and arrange it on top of the sauce, then top with the artichoke hearts and fried onion.

4. Heat the pizzas under the grill for a few minutes until they are piping hot and the cheese is melted and lightly browned.

SERVES 2–4

GORGONZOLA AND WALNUT PIZZA

1 oval or round granary loaf (400g / 14oz)	**125g / 4oz Gorgonzola cheese**
olive oil	**50g / 2oz walnut pieces**
tomato sauce (see opposite)	

1. Cut the granary loaf horizontally in half, scoop out a little of the crumb, then brush the inside with olive oil and and toast it under the grill. Toast both sides if you want a crisp pizza base.

2. Heat the tomato sauce then spread this evenly over the bread. Slice the cheese and arrange it on top of the sauce, then top with the walnuts.

3. Heat the pizzas under the grill for a few minutes until they are piping hot and the cheese is melted and lightly browned.

SERVES 2–4

PESTO PIZZA

1 ciabatta loaf	**2–4 tbls pesto sauce**
olive oil	**a few black olives (optional)**
tomato sauce (see opposite)	
75g / 3oz Parmesan cheese	

1. Cut the loaf horizontally in half, brush each cut surface with olive oil and toast it under the grill. Toast both sides if you want a crisp pizza base.

2. Heat the tomato sauce then spread it over the bread. Slice the cheese into thin slivers and arrange on top of the sauce, then drizzle the pesto over everything and add the olives if you're using these.

3. Heat the pizzas under the grill for a few minutes until they are piping hot and the cheese is melted and lightly browned.

SERVES 2–4

Bottled pesto is readily available nowadays, and some Italian delicatessens and large supermarkets stock fresh pesto sauce. If you have time, you might like to make your own (see page 59).

TWO-CHEESE PIZZA

2 muffins
125g / 4oz Mozzarella
  cheese
50g / 2oz Parmesan
  cheese

12 black olives
tomato sauce (see
  page 16)

Light rolls or baps, or pieces of French stick or ciabatta bread, split in half, also make good bases for these toppings.

1. Cut the muffins in half and toast them on both sides under the grill.
2. Meanwhile, thinly slice the cheeses and halve and stone the olives.
3. Heat the tomato sauce and spread it over the muffins, then top with the slices of cheese and the olives.
4. Heat the pizzas under the grill for a few minutes until they are piping hot and the cheese is golden brown and bubbling.

SERVES 2

SWEETCORN AND CHERRY TOMATO PIZZA

2 muffins
125g / 4oz Cheddar
  cheese
6 cherry tomatoes
tomato sauce (see
  page 16)

50g / 2oz canned or
  frozen sweetcorn
  kernels
salt and freshly
  ground black pepper

1. Cut the muffins in half and toast them on both sides under the grill.
2. Meanwhile, grate the cheese and slice the cherry tomatoes.
3. Heat the tomato sauce and spread it evenly over the muffins, then top with the grated cheese, sweetcorn and cherry tomatoes. Season with salt and pepper.
4. Heat the pizzas under the grill for a few minutes until they are piping hot and the cheese is golden brown and bubbling.

SERVES 2

RED PEPPER, AUBERGINE AND GOAT'S CHEESE PIZZA

1 small red pepper
1 medium aubergine
olive oil
2 muffins
tomato sauce (see
  page 16)

salt and freshly
  ground black pepper
50g / 2oz goat's cheese
  log

1. Cut the pepper into quarters then put it cut-side down on a grill pan. Cut the aubergine into slices about 3 mm / ⅛ inch thick and lay these on the grill pan too. Brush the aubergine slices on both sides with olive oil then grill on high for 5–10 minutes, until the skin on the pepper is blistered and charred in places and the aubergine is golden brown and tender. Remove from the grill but leave it on. Cover the pepper with a damp cloth.
2. Cut the muffins in half and toast them on both sides under the grill.
3. Heat the tomato sauce then spread it over the muffins and top with the aubergine slices. Remove the loose skin and seeds from the pepper, cut it into long, thin strips and arrange on top of the aubergine. Season with salt and pepper.
4. Break off small pieces of goat's cheese and dot them over the top of the pizzas. Grind a little black pepper coarsely over the goat's cheese then heat the pizzas under the grill for a few minutes until they are piping hot.

SERVES 2

OPPOSITE: *Two-Cheese Pizza, Sweetcorn and Cherry Tomato Pizza, Red Pepper, Aubergine and Goat's Cheese Pizza*

SNACKS ON TOAST
✳

TOASTED CHEESE

This simple version of cheese on toast is quick and easy to make and you can vary it by using different types of bread and cheese, substituting beer, wine or cider for the milk, and adding extra ingredients such as tomatoes, onion, herbs, mushrooms, chutney or pickle – whatever takes your fancy.

1–2 slices of bread	*1–2 tbls milk*
75–125g / 3–4oz	*freshly ground black*
Cheddar cheese,	*pepper*
grated	

1 Preheat the grill and toast the bread on one side.
2 Mix the cheese with the milk to make a paste then season with freshly ground black pepper.
3 Spread the cheese mixture on the untoasted side of the bread, grill until puffed up and golden brown then serve at once.
SERVES 1

VARIATIONS

1 WITH ASPARAGUS

This is an extremely nice variation if you are making toasted cheese for more than one person and want something that is extra special. Allow about 3–4 asparagus spears per person, trim them then cut them into 2.5 cm/1 inch lengths and cook in boiling water for 2–4 minutes, until just tender. Drain and serve heaped on top of the toasted cheese.

2 WITH CIDER AND APPLES

Use cider instead of the milk. Peel and core a small, mellow eating apple such as Cox's, then cut it into thin rings or slices and arrange it on the toast. Cover with the cheese mixture and grill until the cheese is puffed up and golden brown and the apple is tender.

3 WITH OLIVES

I like this best made with feta cheese, which you can crumble rather than grate. Add 6–8 black or green olives, or a mixture of both, to the cheese.

4 WITH ONION AND MUSTARD

Mix the cheese with beer instead of milk and add ½–1 teaspoon of made mustard and 1 finely chopped small onion.

5 WITH CHILLI

De-seed and finely chop 1 small green chilli and add it to the grated cheese.

MOZZARELLA IN CARROZZA

Use the best Mozzarella you can find – certainly one packed in water – for this delicious mixture of hot melting cheese and crisp fried bread.

125g / 4oz Mozzarella	*2 eggs*
cheese	*olive oil*
4 slices of bread, crusts	
removed	

1 Drain and slice the cheese and sandwich it between the slices of bread, pressing them firmly together.
2 Lightly beat the eggs, then strain them into a shallow dish. Put the sandwiches in the egg and leave them for a few minutes to soak it up, turning them over once.
3 Heat a little olive oil in a frying pan and fry the sandwiches on both sides until they are golden brown and crisp. Drain them quickly on kitchen paper and serve at once.
SERVES 2

Mozzarella in Carrozza means 'Mozzarella in a carriage', a poetic and apt description.

BUTTERY SCRAMBLED
EGGS ON TOAST

2 slices of bread   salt and freshly
butter   ground black pepper
4 eggs

1. Toast the bread, butter it and keep it warm.
2. Lightly beat the eggs and season with salt and pepper.
3. Melt a knob of butter in a saucepan. When it sizzles, add the eggs and cook over a low heat for a few minutes, stirring.
4. Just before the eggs set, move the pan from the heat and, to make the scrambled eggs extra delicious, stir in a few slivers of butter. The eggs will continue to cook in the heat of the pan.
5. Pile the scrambled eggs on to the toast and serve at once on warmed plates.
SERVES 2

VARIATIONS

1 WITH FRESH HERBS

Add 1–2 tablespoons of chopped fresh herbs at the end of the cooking time, along with the extra butter.

2 PIPERADE

Piperade takes longer to cook than plain scrambled eggs but it is nice when you want something a bit more substantial.

Melt 25g/1oz butter in a pan then add 1 large onion, peeled and chopped, and 1 green pepper, de-seeded and chopped. Cover and cook for 10 minutes, until soft but not browned, then add 450g/1lb tomatoes, skinned and chopped, and 1 clove of garlic, crushed. Cook gently, uncovered, for about 10 minutes, until the vegetables are soft but not mushy. Meanwhile, toast and butter 4 slices of granary or wholewheat bread, cut it into fingers and keep it warm. Lightly beat 4 eggs then pour them into the pan with the vegetables and stir gently until they begin to set. Remove from the heat (the eggs will continue to cook in the heat of the pan), season and serve immediately with the toast fingers.

CLUB SANDWICH

3 slices of wholewheat   ½ small avocado
   bread   salt and freshly
butter   ground black pepper
2 lettuce leaves   4 cocktail sticks
1 small tomato, sliced   4 stuffed olives
mayonnaise or
   mustard

1. Toast the bread, butter one piece and arrange the lettuce, tomato and a little mayonnaise or mustard on top.
2. Cover with another piece of toast, buttered on both sides. Peel, stone and slice the avocado, arrange on top of the toast and season with salt and pepper.
3. Butter the third piece of toast and place, butter-side down, on top of the avocado. Press down on the sandwich, cut it into quarters then spear each quarter with a cocktail stick and decorate with a stuffed olive.
SERVES 1

CAMEMBERT TOAST
WITH APRICOT JAM

I love the combination of Camembert cheese and something sweet. If you find the jam too sweet, however, mango chutney is also very good.

1 slice of wholewheat   2–3 tsp good-quality
   bread   apricot jam
2 portions of   2–3 tsp chopped
   Camembert cheese   hazelnuts

1. Heat the grill and toast the bread on both sides.
2. Mash the Camembert roughly on the toast then put some dollops of apricot jam on top of that.
3. Grill until the cheese has melted then sprinkle with the nuts and grill again until lightly browned.
SERVES 1

A good way of using up the other half of the avocado is to make guacamole; mash the avocado with 1 skinned, chopped tomato and some finely chopped chilli; then add plenty of chopped fresh coriander and season to taste.

OPEN SANDWICHES & PAN BAGNAT
— ✳ —

RADICCHIO AND CREAM CHEESE

75g / 3oz cream cheese
 or curd cheese
2 slices of dark rye
 bread
a few radicchio leaves

2 dill-pickled
 cucumbers, sliced
sprigs of fresh dill
 (optional)

1. Spread about half of the cream or curd cheese on the bread, then press the radicchio leaves on top of that.
2. Spoon the remaining cheese on top, then arrange slices of dill-pickled cucumber on top of that and finish with a sprig of fresh dill, if you like.
SERVES 2

BRIE AND RED ONION

mayonnaise
2 slices of wholewheat
 bread
2–4 little gem lettuce
 leaves

50g / 2oz Brie
3–4 slices of red onion
a few walnuts

1. Spread a thin layer of mayonnaise on the bread then arrange the lettuce on top, pressing it down into the mayonnaise to make it stick.
2. Slice the Brie thinly then arrange it on top of the lettuce with the red onion slices and sprinkle with a few walnuts.
SERVES 2

You can vary the filling for pan bagnat according to your taste and what is available: try adding slices of cheese, or cream cheese, hummus with some olives, or any of the fillings for pitta pockets (see pages 24-5). The main thing is to be generous with the filling.

EGG AND OLIVE

2 slices of white
 poppyseed bread
mayonnaise
4 frisée lettuce leaves

1 hard-boiled egg
6 black olives
paprika pepper

1. Spread the bread with a thin layer of mayonnaise then arrange the lettuce on top.
2. Chop the hard-boiled egg into chunks and mix with a little mayonnaise to moisten. Divide this mixture between the bread slices and garnish with the olives and a little paprika.
SERVES 2

PAN BAGNAT

1 long French stick
450g / 1lb tomatoes
salt and freshly ground
 black pepper
1 lettuce

225g / 8oz Mozzarella
 cheese
1 large avocado
lemon juice
fresh basil leaves

1. Cut the French stick into quarters. Slice each piece open and scoop out most of the crumb.
2. Slice the tomatoes and sprinkle with salt. Wash the lettuce and spin or pat dry; slice the Mozzarella cheese; stone, peel and slice the avocado and sprinkle the slices with lemon juice, salt and pepper.
3. Fill the bread with layers of the ingredients, adding torn basil leaves and seasoning to each layer. If you are eating the sandwiches later, wrap them tightly and keep in the fridge until needed.
SERVES 4

OPPOSITE: (top) Pan Bagnat and (bottom) Open Sandwiches

PITTA POCKETS
※

Pitta breads make very convenient containers for all kinds of delicious ingredients that would be too moist or bulky to put in a sandwich. Salads and stir-fries can be piled into warmed pitta pockets; grilled vegetables, too, freshly cooked and still sizzling; and simple mixtures of beans, vegetables, cheese and hummus. Here is a selection of fillings.

You can sprinkle the aubergine with salt, leave it for 30 minutes, then rinse it if you wish; this isn't usually necessary as a precaution against bitterness, but it can reduce the amount of oil the aubergine absorbs.

SPICED CHICK PEAS

A tomato, sliced into quarters or eighths, is nice added to this for a change.

1 onion, peeled and finely chopped
2 tbls olive oil
2 garlic cloves, crushed
1 tsp cumin seeds
1 × 425g / 15oz can chick peas, drained
2 pitta breads

4–6 lettuce leaves
4 tbls thick Greek yogurt, or a mixture of yogurt and good-quality mayonnaise
salt and freshly ground black pepper
paprika pepper

1 Fry the onion in the oil, with a lid on the pan, for 5 minutes. Stir in the garlic and cumin seeds, cover again and cook for a further 2–3 minutes until the onion is tender.

2 Add the chick peas to the onion and cook for 4–5 minutes, until heated through and perhaps lightly browned in places.

3 Warm the pitta breads under the grill then cut them lengthwise in half. Gently open up each half and put in the lettuce, tearing it as necessary, then spoon in the chick pea mixture. Season the yogurt or yogurt and mayonnaise, spoon on top of the chick peas and sprinkle with a little paprika pepper. Serve at once.
SERVES 2

AUBERGINE WITH PESTO

1 large aubergine
olive oil
2 pitta breads
1–2 tbls good-quality bought pesto sauce, or home-made (see page 59)

salt and freshly ground black pepper

1 Heat the grill. Cut the aubergine lengthwise into slices about 3 mm/⅛ inch thick and lay these on a grill pan. Brush the slices on both sides with olive oil then grill on high for 5–10 minutes, turning them over as necessary, until golden brown and tender.

2 Warm the pitta breads under the grill, then cut them lengthwise in half and gently open up each half. Mix the aubergine slices with pesto to taste, season, then spoon them into the pitta breads and serve at once.
SERVES 2

GREEK SALAD

4–6 lettuce leaves
small piece of cucumber
2 small tomatoes
4 spring onions
a few black olives, stoned
2 tbls olive oil

2 tsp wine vinegar
salt and freshly ground black pepper
125g / 4oz feta cheese
chopped fresh mint or oregano
2 pitta breads

1. Wash the salad ingredients then tear the lettuce, dice the cucumber, slice the tomatoes, chop the spring onions and put them into a bowl. Add the olives, oil, vinegar and a grinding of pepper.
2. Cut the feta into cubes and mix it with the other ingredients, then add the fresh mint or oregano and a little salt if necessary.
3. Warm the pitta breads through under the grill, then cut them lengthwise in half, gently open up each half and fill with the feta mixture.
SERVES 2

COUSCOUS, TOMATO AND MINT

125g / 4oz couscous	juice of 1 lemon
50g / 2oz raisins (optional)	4 tbls chopped fresh mint
2 spring onions	salt and freshly ground black pepper
4 tomatoes	
2 pitta breads	

1. Put the couscous and the raisins, if you are using them, into a bowl and cover with boiling water. Leave on one side for 10 minutes.
2. Meanwhile, trim and chop the spring onions, chop the tomatoes and warm the pitta breads under the grill.
3. Drain the couscous and mix with the spring onions, tomatoes, lemon juice, mint and salt and pepper to taste.
4. Split the pitta breads lengthwise in half, gently open each half and fill with the couscous mixture.
SERVES 2

RED BEAN AND SWEETCORN

2 tbls olive oil	1 × 200g / 7oz can sweetcorn, drained
1 small onion, peeled and chopped	1 × 225g / 8oz can red kidney beans, drained
1 small green pepper, chopped	salt and freshly ground black pepper
1 × 200g / 7oz can tomatoes	2 pitta breads

1. Heat the oil in a pan, put in the onion and pepper, cover and cook gently for 10 minutes, or until they are getting tender.
2. Mash in the tomatoes with their juice, cover and cook for a further 10 minutes, then add the sweetcorn and kidney beans. Cook gently for a few more minutes until hot. Season with salt and pepper.
3. Warm the pitta breads under the grill, then cut them lengthwise in half, gently open up each half, fill with the red bean mixture and serve at once.
SERVES 2

CHEESE AND CARROT VINAIGRETTE

2 carrots (about 225g / 8oz)	2 tbls olive oil
125g / 4oz Cheddar cheese	2 tsp wine vinegar
4 spring onions	salt and freshly ground black pepper
	2 pitta breads

1. Scrape or peel the carrots then coarsely grate the carrots and cheese into a bowl. Trim and slice the spring onions and add them to the bowl, together with the oil, vinegar and a seasoning of salt and pepper. Mix well.
2. Warm the pitta breads under the grill, then cut them lengthwise in half, gently open up each half, fill with the carrot mixture and serve at once.
SERVES 2

You could use bulgur wheat instead of couscous for a change: prepare it in the same way.

TORTILLAS & POPPADUMS

---------------- ✳ ----------------

TORTILLA SALAD ROLLS

2 tortillas
6–8 iceberg lettuce
  leaves
2 tomatoes
small piece of
  cucumber
2 spring onions

4 tbls mayonnaise,
  soured cream, yogurt
  or a mixture
hot chilli sauce such
  as Tabasco
salt and freshly
  ground black pepper

1 Put the tortillas into a frying pan over a moderate heat, one at a time, to warm through, or heat them under the grill.

2 Shred the lettuce leaves and chop the tomatoes, cucumber and spring onions. Mix with the mayonnaise, soured cream or yogurt then add a dash of hot chilli sauce and some salt and pepper to taste.

3 Spread the salad mixture on to the warm tortillas, roll them up firmly and serve at once.
SERVES 2

POPPADUMS WITH AVOCADO AND CURRIED MAYONNAISE

2 tsp curry powder
2 tbls mayonnaise
2 tbls plain yogurt
1 tsp mango chutney
salt and freshly
  ground black pepper

1 avocado
2 tomatoes
squeeze of lemon juice
2–3 poppadums
paprika pepper or
  fresh coriander

OPPOSITE: (top) Poppadums with Avocado and Curried Mayonnaise and (bottom) Pitta Pockets with (left) Cheese and Carrot Vinaigrette and (right) Red Bean and Sweetcorn, page 25

1 Put the curry powder into a dry saucepan and heat for 1–2 minutes until it smells aromatic. Remove from the heat and mix with the mayonnaise, yogurt, chutney and salt and pepper to taste.

2 Peel, stone and chop the avocado then put it in a bowl. Dice the tomatoes and add to the avocado with the lemon juice and salt and pepper to taste.

3 Put the poppadums on a plate, spoon the avocado mixture on the side and trickle the curried mayonnaise over it. Finish with a sprinkling of paprika pepper or a little chopped fresh coriander.
SERVES 1

RED BEAN BURRITOS

2 onions, peeled and
  chopped
2 tbls olive oil
2 garlic cloves, crushed
1 chilli, de-seeded and
  chopped
1 tsp cumin seeds
2 tomatoes

1 × 425g / 15oz can red
  kidney beans, drained
2 tbls chopped fresh
  coriander
salt and freshly ground
  black pepper
2 tortillas
soured cream to serve

1 Fry the onions in the oil, with a lid on the pan, for 5 minutes. Add the garlic, chilli and cumin and cook for 1–2 minutes.

2 Cover the tomatoes with boiling water for a few seconds, then drain and slip off the skins. Chop and add to the pan with the kidney beans. Cook gently for 5 minutes or until heated through, mashing the beans to make a rough purée. Add the coriander and season with salt and pepper.

3 Warm the tortillas one at a time in a frying pan over a moderate heat, or heat them under the grill. Spread the bean mixture on the warm tortillas, roll them up and serve with soured cream.
SERVES 2

The tortillas that you can now buy make a good fast-food snack, warmed through, filled with tasty ingredients and then rolled up. They can be eaten immediately or topped with grated cheese and put under a hot grill to melt the cheese. The remaining tortillas will keep well in a polythene bag in the freezer.

CROISSANTS, ROLLS & SWEET IDEAS

SPEEDY GARLIC BREAD

Although garlic bread is usually made in the oven, you can speed things up by using the grill instead.

½ French stick or 2 crusty rolls, white or wholewheat
2 garlic cloves, crushed

50g / 2oz butter, softened

1 Heat the grill. Cut the French stick on the diagonal into slices about 2.5 cm/1 inch thick, or cut the rolls in half.
2 Mix together the garlic and butter then spread this over the cut surfaces of the bread.
3 Grill the bread until hot and sizzling on one side, then turn it over to heat the other side. Serve immediately, or cover with foil and keep warm.
SERVES 2

CREAMY ASPARAGUS CROISSANTS

This delicious snack for one is rather like a cheat's version of feuilleté of asparagus in cream.

125–225g / 4–8oz asparagus spears
15g / ½ oz butter
1½ tsp cornflour
150ml / 5fl oz single cream

salt and freshly ground black pepper
freshly grated nutmeg
2 croissants

1 Trim the asparagus as necessary and cut it into 2.5 cm/1 inch lengths. Keep the tips separate from the stems.
2 Cook the chopped stems in 2.5 cm/1 inch of boiling water for 2 minutes, then add the tips and cook for a further 2 minutes, until they are beginning to get tender but are still crunchy. Drain.
3 Melt the butter in a pan and stir in the cornflour. Add the cream and stir over a moderate heat until it comes to the boil and thickens. Cook for 1–2 minutes then remove from the heat and stir in the asparagus. Season with salt, pepper and nutmeg.
4 Slice the croissant horizontally in half. Grill on both sides until crisp and lightly browned.
5 Serve the croissant halves with the asparagus, sandwiching them together with the mixture if you like, and letting the excess run on to the plate.
SERVES 2

GARLIC MUSHROOM ROLL

175g / 6oz button mushrooms
15g / ½ oz butter
1 tsp olive oil
1–2 garlic cloves, crushed

salt and freshly ground black pepper
1 high, rounded, crusty roll, white or granary

1 Wash and roughly chop the mushrooms, then fry them in the butter and olive oil for 5 minutes or until they are tender. If they give off a lot of liquid, go on cooking them until this has evaporated; this may take as long as 10 minutes.
2 Add the garlic and cook for 1–2 minutes longer. Season with salt and pepper.
3 Meanwhile, heat the grill. Slice the top off the roll to make a lid; scoop out and discard most of the crumb. Warm through the roll and lid under the grill, turning it.
4 Spoon the mushrooms into the roll and replace the lid. Serve at once.
SERVES 1

Cheese and Garlic Bread makes a nice variation: simply put slivers of cheese (such as Gruyère) on the garlic bread before grilling it; or try herb bread, using 1 tablespoon of chopped fresh parsley and chives instead of, or as well as, the garlic.

CHUTNEY BEAN BURGER

Use whatever chutney or pickle you like in this; you could also add extras such as grated cheese, mustard, mayonnaise, sliced tomato and lettuce to make a kind of burger with everything.

1 onion, peeled and
  chopped
1 tbls olive oil
1 garlic clove, crushed
1 × 225g / 8oz can
  butter beans, drained

1–2 tbls chutney or
  pickle
salt and freshly
  ground black pepper
1 soft burger roll

1   Fry the onion in the olive oil, with a lid on the pan, for 5 minutes. Add the garlic to the pan and cook for 1–2 minutes longer.

2   Add the beans to the pan and cook gently for about 5 minutes, until heated through, mashing the beans to make a rough purée. Stir in the chutney or pickle and season with salt and pepper.

3   Heat the grill. Cut the burger roll in half and warm it through under the grill, then pile the bean mixture on one half, top with the other half, press down and serve immediately.

SERVES 1

BRIOCHE WITH VACHERIN AND APRICOT CONSERVE

An indulgent breakfast, brunch or pudding.

1 individual brioche
125g / 4oz Vacherin
  cheese

1–2 tbls best-quality
  apricot conserve

1   Warm the brioche in the oven or under the grill, then serve with the Vacherin cheese and apricot conserve.

SERVES 1

GINGER AND CREAM CHEESE BAGELS

125g / 4oz cream
  cheese, full fat or
  low fat
2 pieces of preserved
  stem ginger

6 walnut halves
a little milk (optional)
2 bagels

1   Put the cream cheese into a bowl. Chop the ginger and walnuts and beat into the cream cheese, adding a little milk if necessary to soften it.

2   Cut the bagels in half, spread with the filling and sandwich together.

SERVES 2

BAGELS WITH CHOPPED-HERRING-WITHOUT-HERRING

This filling is a piquant and intriguing relish from New Food For All Palates by Sally and Lucian Berg. It also makes a good topping for crostini or bruschetta.

25g / 1oz white bread,
  crusts removed
7 tsp white wine
  vinegar
2 eggs, hard-boiled
40g / 1½oz mild onion
25g / 1oz green pepper

25g / 1oz peeled sharp
  apple
1 rounded tsp sea salt
4 tsp olive oil
white pepper
2 bagels

1   Tear the bread into pieces, put these into a bowl and sprinkle with the vinegar.

2   Shell the eggs, chop them roughly and put them into a food processor with the onion, green pepper and apple, also in rough chunks. Add the bread, salt and oil and whizz to a chunky purée. Season, adding some white pepper to taste.

3   Cut the bagels in half, spread the filling over them and sandwich together.

SERVES 2

PANETTONE WITH FRESH FIGS

This makes a good quick festive pudding. Other fruits such as clementines, peeled and sliced, could be substituted for the figs, or instead of the fresh fruit you could use fruits preserved in alcohol.

6–8 fresh figs
4 slices of panettone
1 tub of thick Greek yogurt

a few flaked almonds

1. Wash and slice the figs, then arrange them on individual plates with a slice of panettone, a good dollop of Greek yogurt and a few flaked almonds.
SERVES 4

CINNAMON TOAST WITH HONEYED APPLES

Rather like an apple charlotte, this is a pleasant combination of crisp, sugary cinnamon toast and buttery apple slices. The recipe also works well with pears instead of apples, and white bread rather than brown. Some chilled thick yogurt or pouring cream makes a good accompaniment.

2 sweet, mellow eating apples, such as Cox's
butter
2 tbls honey
2–4 slices of white bread

2–4 tbls demerara sugar
ground cinnamon

1. Peel the apples, cut them into quarters, remove the cores, then cut each quarter into thin slices.
2. Heat a little butter in a saucepan and add the apples and honey. Cook, uncovered, over a gentle heat, until the apple slices have softened, about 3–4 minutes, stirring gently from time to time.

3. Meanwhile, make the cinnamon toast: toast the bread on both sides – don't get it too brown and crisp. Remove the crusts if you like, then butter the toast. Cover each slice evenly with demerara sugar and sprinkle with cinnamon.
4. Put the toast under the grill for 1–2 minutes until the sugar has melted a bit to make a crisp coating. Cut into fingers or triangles.
5. Spoon the apple slices on to a small plate and arrange the cinnamon toast around them.
SERVES 2

CROISSANT WITH CREAM AND BLACK CHERRY CONSERVE

Unless a croissant is superb in flavour and texture, I think that halving and grilling it is by far the nicest way to serve it – either with butter or with a sweet or savoury filling. Here, a combination of three of my favourite foods makes an indulgent occasional treat.

1 croissant
1–2 tbls black cherry conserve
1–2 tbls thick double cream, crème fraîche or soured cream

a little icing sugar (optional)

1. Slice the croissant in half horizontally. Grill on both sides until crisp and lightly browned.
2. Spread the bottom half with black cherry conserve, cover with the cream, then replace the top half of the croissant.
3. Sift a little icing sugar over, if you like.
SERVES 1

OPPOSITE: *(left) Panettone with Fresh Figs, (top) Croissant with Cream and Black Cherry Conserve, (right) Cinnamon Toast with Honeyed Apples*

EGGS, CHEESE
& DAIRY FOODS

*These foods are easy to turn into a quick feast,
with dishes such as Tortilla, Spinach and Stilton
Crêpes, Haloumi with Spiced Leeks or Chocolate
Amaretti Pudding. Cheese is perfect for simple
instant meals – see No-Cook Cheese Feasts for
ideas – and yogurt, soft cheeses and cream form
the basis of quick and easy desserts. Dairy
products do contain fat, but used in moderation
and balanced with vegetables, fruit and cereals
they definitely have a place in a healthy,
fast-food diet.*

OMELETTES
*

SUN-DRIED TOMATO AND HERB OMELETTE

2 eggs
4 sun-dried tomatoes
in oil, drained
2 tbls chopped fresh
herbs, such as chervil,
chives and parsley

salt and freshly
ground black pepper
15g / ½ oz butter

1 Break the eggs into a bowl and beat them lightly until just combined. Chop the sun-dried tomatoes and add to the eggs, together with the herbs. Season with salt and pepper.
2 Put a 15 cm/6 inch frying pan over a medium heat. When it is hot add the butter, turn the heat up and swirl the butter around – don't let it brown.
3 Pour in the eggs, tilting the pan to distribute them evenly, then, using a fork, draw the set edges towards the centre and let the liquid egg run to the edges. Repeat until the omelette is almost set.
4 Tilt the pan over a warmed plate, then fold the edge of the omelette over to the centre and let it fold over again on to the plate. Serve immediately.
SERVES 1

VARIATIONS

1 CHEESE AND HERB

Grate 40g/1½ oz Gruyère cheese and add half to the beaten eggs instead of the tomatoes. When the omelette is almost set, sprinkle the remaining cheese over the centre.

2 FRESH TOMATO

Skin, de-seed and chop 1 large tomato, warm it through in a little butter in a small pan and season. When the omelette is almost set, spoon the tomato over the centre. You could add some slivers of spring onion, or some fresh basil or other herbs, too, if you like. Turn out the omelette and serve dusted with finely grated fresh Parmesan cheese.

SOUFFLE OMELETTE

Halfway between a soufflé and an omelette (though far quicker to cook than a soufflé) a soufflé omelette makes a pleasant change and can be served with sweet or savoury fillings.

2 eggs, separated
salt and freshly
ground black pepper
(for a savoury
omelette)

15g / ½ oz butter

1 Heat the grill. Put the egg yolks into a bowl, add 2 tablespoons of water, and some seasoning if you're making a savoury omelette, and mix well.
2 Whisk the egg whites until they stand in stiff peaks, but don't let them get too dry. Stir a spoonful of beaten egg white into the yolks, then gently fold in the rest with a metal spoon.
3 Heat a 15 cm/6 inch frying pan over a moderate heat then put in the butter and tilt the pan so that the butter coats the sides. Pour the egg mixture into the pan and cook over a moderate heat for 1–2 minutes, until golden brown underneath. Put the pan under the grill for 1–2 minutes to brown the top of the omelette.
4 Cut across the centre of the omelette (don't cut right through it), spoon your chosen filling (see below) over one half, then fold over the other half. Lift the omelette out of the pan and serve.
SERVES 1

SAVOURY FILLINGS

1 ASPARAGUS

Boil or steam 2–4 asparagus spears until just tender then cut them into 2.5 cm/1 inch lengths.

2 PEPPER

Grill ½ red or yellow pepper, or a combination, until charred then peel off the skin and slice thinly.

If you are making a sweet soufflé omelette, for a flashy finish fill the omelette with your chosen mixture, fold it in half, then sift 2 tablespoons of icing sugar over the top and caramelise the sugar by laying a red-hot skewer on top for a moment or two in a criss-cross pattern.

3 MUSHROOM

Wash, dry and slice 50g/2oz mushrooms – any type, or a mixture – then sauté them in 15g/½ oz butter until they are tender and any liquid they produce has boiled away (this may take up to 15 minutes). Season with salt and pepper.

4 CHEESE

Mix 2 tablespoons of grated cheese with the egg yolks, then sprinkle another 2 tablespoons on top of the omelette just before you fold it. Gruyère or Parmesan, or a mixture, are good.

5 RATATOUILLE

Leftover ratatouille (see page 40) makes a very good filling; reheat gently, allowing 2 heaped tablespoons per omelette.

6 TRUFFLE

For a luxurious treat, put a few truffle shavings on top of the omelette before folding it.

7 PETITS POIS AND MINT

Cook 50g/2oz fresh or frozen petits pois in a little boiling water for 2 minutes. Drain, add a knob of butter and 2 teaspoons of chopped fresh mint.

SWEET FILLINGS

1 FRESH FRUIT

Any sweet, soft-textured fruit is good, such as blackberries or blueberries, sliced sweet ripe mango, or sliced banana with a sprinkling of cinnamon. Or use 50g/2oz strawberries or other red berries, sliced and sprinkled with sugar and 1 tablespoon of liqueur: try Cointreau with strawberries or kirsch with cherries.

2 JAM

Melt 1 tablespoon of jam in a small pan over a gentle heat – apricot or black cherry are especially good. You could also add a dash of liqueur.

3 PRESERVED FRUIT

Use 2 tablespoons of fruits preserved in liqueur, or coarsely chopped stem ginger.

TORTILLA

This simple Spanish omelette is wonderfully tasty and filling, and like all flat omelettes it can be eaten hot, warm or cold. Any that's left over is delicious the next day, reheated and served with a fresh tomato sauce or served hot or cold with salad.

900g / 2lb potatoes	*3 tbls olive oil*
1 large onion or 1	*salt and freshly ground*
bunch of spring	*black pepper*
onions	*6 eggs*

1 Half fill a saucepan with water and put it on the stove to heat up. Peel the potatoes, cut them into chunks about 1 cm/½ inch square then add them to the pan and boil for 6–8 minutes or until just tender. Drain and set aside.

2 Meanwhile, peel and chop the onion or trim and chop the spring onions. Heat 2 tablespoons of the olive oil in a 20 cm/8 inch frying pan then put in the onion. Cover and cook until tender: 7–8 minutes for the onion, 2–3 minutes for the spring onions.

3 Add the potatoes to the frying pan, stirring to mix all the ingredients together and adding some salt and pepper to taste. Leave the vegetables to cook gently while you beat the eggs with a little salt and pepper.

4 Pour the eggs into the frying pan. Cook the tortilla gently until it is lightly browned underneath and looks set on top, about 5–10 minutes.

5 Invert a large plate over the frying pan and turn the tortilla out on to it. Heat the remaining oil in the pan then slide the tortilla back in to cook the other side: this will take about 3–4 minutes. Serve cut into wedges.
SERVES 4

VARIATION

MIXED VEGETABLE TORTILLA

De-seed and chop 1 green pepper and fry it with the onion. Boil 125g/4oz frozen peas with the potatoes, adding them a couple of minutes before the end of the cooking time.

Tortilla makes a good appetizer, cut into small squares and accompanied by a spicy dipping sauce.

SWISS CHARD TORTILLA

6 eggs
125g / 4oz cheese,
  grated (Parmesan,
  Gruyère or a mixture)
3–4 tbls chopped fresh
  basil or parsley

salt and freshly
  ground black pepper
3 tbls olive oil
225g / 8oz Swiss chard,
  without stalks

1 Beat the eggs and stir in three quarters of the cheese, plus the herbs and some salt and pepper.

2 Heat 2 tablespoons of the olive oil in a large saucepan, put in the chard and stir-fry for 1–2 minutes until wilted. Be careful not to let it burn.

3 Heat the remaining oil in a 20 cm/8 inch frying pan and tip in the chard, spreading it over the pan – it will still be very springy and leafy. Then pour the eggs on top of the leaves. Check that the mixture isn't sticking to the bottom of the pan then cover and cook over the lowest possible heat for about 15 minutes, until set.

4 Heat the grill. Sprinkle the remaining cheese over the tortilla and place under the grill for 1–2 minutes to cook the top. Serve cut into wedges.
SERVES 4

SUMMER FRITTATA

225g / 8oz tender
  asparagus spears
225g / 8oz courgettes
8 sun-dried tomatoes
  in oil, drained
4 eggs
25g / 1oz Parmesan
  cheese, grated

2 tbls chopped fresh
  parsley
salt and freshly
  ground black pepper
2 tbls olive oil

OPPOSITE: *(left) Cheese and Herb Omelette, page 34, (top) Mushroom Soufflé Omelette, page 35, (right) Vegetable Frittata with Mint Sauce*

1 Trim the asparagus and cut the courgettes into 6 mm/¼ inch slices. Cook the vegetables in a little boiling water for a few minutes until tender but slightly crunchy. Drain immediately.

2 Heat the grill. Chop the sun-dried tomatoes. Whisk the eggs lightly, add the cheese, tomatoes and parsley and season with a little salt and pepper.

3 Heat the oil in a 20 cm/8 inch frying pan, add the vegetables then pour in the egg mixture. Cook for 4–5 minutes, until the bottom of the frittata is set and golden brown, then put the frying pan under the grill and leave for a further minute or two to set the top. Serve cut in half or in thick wedges.
SERVES 2

VEGETABLE FRITTATA WITH MINT SAUCE

225g / 8oz cauliflower
1 carrot
125g / 4oz petits pois
4 eggs
salt and freshly
  ground black pepper

15g / ½ oz butter

FOR THE MINT SAUCE
25g / 1oz mint
1 tbls honey
1 tbls wine vinegar

1 First make the mint sauce: wash the mint and remove any tough stems, then chop the leaves in a food processor or by hand and add the honey and vinegar. Put into a bowl to serve with the frittata.

2 Wash the cauliflower and cut it into florets then scrape and slice the carrot. Cook the vegetables in 5 cm/2 inches of boiling water for about 4 minutes, until just tender, then drain and return to the still-warm pan. Stir in the peas.

3 Heat the grill. Whisk the eggs lightly and season with salt and pepper.

4 Melt the butter in a 20 cm/8 inch frying pan, add the vegetables then pour in the eggs. Cook for 4–5 minutes, until set and golden brown underneath, then put under the grill for 1–2 minutes to set the top. Serve cut into wedges, with the mint sauce.
SERVES 2

You won't need the thick, juicy stalks from the chard for this recipe: these are excellent cooked in boiling water until just tender then served with butter and/or shavings of Parmesan, or in a light cheese sauce. If you can't get Swiss chard you can make the tortilla with spinach.

CREPES

❋

BASIC CREPE RECIPE

125g / 4oz plain flour – white or half white and half wholewheat
2 eggs
2 tbls oil or melted butter, plus extra for frying

300ml / ½ pint skimmed milk or milk and water

1 If you've got a liquidizer or food processor, put in the flour, eggs, oil or melted butter and milk and whizz to a batter. If not, put the flour into a bowl and beat in the eggs, oil or butter and about a third of the milk. Mix until smooth, then gradually beat in the rest of the milk. The batter should be the consistency of single cream.

2 Put a 15 cm/6 inch frying pan over a low heat and brush it with a little oil or melted butter: a good way to do this is with a pad of kitchen paper.

3 When the pan is hot enough to sizzle if a drop of water is flicked into it, pour in 2 tablespoons of batter and tilt the pan until the base is thinly coated.

4 Fry for 1–2 minutes until the top is set then, using a palette knife and your fingers, flip the crêpe over and cook the other side for a few seconds. Cook the remaining crêpes in the same way, brushing the pan with oil or butter between every couple of crêpes. As the crêpes are done, stack them up on a plate, cover them with another plate and keep them warm over a pan of steaming water.
SERVES 4

VARIATIONS

1 HERB CREPES

Add 2 tablespoons of chopped fresh herbs to the batter.

2 ORANGE OR LEMON CREPES

Add the grated rind of 1 orange or lemon and 1 tablespoon of caster sugar to the batter.

3 CHOCOLATE CREPES

Mix 1 tablespoon of cocoa powder and 1 tablespoon of caster sugar in with the batter ingredients.

SPINACH AND STILTON CREPES

crêpe batter (see above)
900g / 2lb fresh spinach

225g / 8oz Stilton cheese
salt and freshly ground black pepper

1 Make the crêpes as described above.

2 Wash the spinach, then cook it in a dry pan for about 7–10 minutes, until it is tender. Drain well.

3 Heat the grill. Crumble or grate the cheese and add half to the spinach, then season with salt and pepper. Spread a little of this mixture on to each crêpe and roll it up. Put the crêpes side by side in a shallow heatproof dish then sprinkle with the rest of the cheese.

4 Put the crêpes under the grill for a few minutes until the cheese on top has melted and everything is bubbling hot. Serve at once.
SERVES 4

VARIATION

CREPES WITH GARLIC AND HERB CREAM CHEESE

Mash 450g/1lb garlic and herb cream cheese with a little milk then spread this on the crêpes and roll them up loosely. Sprinkle with 50g/2oz finely grated Parmesan cheese and brown under the grill.

OPPOSITE: *Crêpes Suzette with Mixed Berries, page 41*

RED CABBAGE, APPLE AND RAISIN CREPES

crêpe batter (see
    page 38)
450g / 1lb red cabbage
1 apple
2 tbls olive oil
1 onion, peeled and
    chopped

salt and freshly
    ground black pepper
50g / 2oz raisins
50g / 2oz Cheddar
    cheese, grated
soured cream
    (optional)

The red cabbage mixture can cook for longer than 15 minutes, if you've got time, and will just go on improving as long as it doesn't stick. If there's any over, it's lovely with baked potatoes and soured cream : in fact, it's almost worth making extra for this!

1. Make the crêpes as described on page 38.
2. Wash the red cabbage and shred it as finely as you can. Chop the apple. Heat the oil in a pan and put in the cabbage, apple and onion. Add a sprinkling of salt and the raisins, cover and cook for 10–15 minutes, until tender. Stir occasionally and add 1–2 tablespoons of water if the mixture starts to stick.
3. Season the cabbage mixture well, then spoon it on to the crêpes and roll them up. Put the crêpes side by side in a shallow heatproof dish then sprinkle over the grated cheese.
4. Put the crêpes under a hot grill for a few minutes until the cheese has melted and everything is bubbling hot. Serve at once, topped with a spoonful of soured cream, if you are using this.

SERVES 4

RATATOUILLE CREPES

herb crêpe batter (see
    page 38)
1 tbls olive oil
1 onion, peeled and
    chopped
1 red pepper
1 aubergine, about
    225–300g / 8–12oz

225g / 8oz courgettes
1 × 400g / 14oz can
    tomatoes
1 garlic clove, crushed
salt and freshly
    ground black pepper
50g / 2oz Parmesan
    cheese, finely grated

1. Make the crêpes as described on page 38.
2. Heat the oil in a pan, add the onion and start to cook this over a moderate heat.
3. Meanwhile, halve, de-seed and chop the red pepper and add this to the onion. Chop the aubergine and the courgettes, and add these to the pan. Finally add the garlic. Cover the pan and cook gently for 5 minutes.
4. Add the tomatoes and their juice, breaking them up with a spoon. Simmer for 15–20 minutes until all the vegetables are tender and the liquid has reduced. Season with salt and pepper then spoon this mixture on to the crêpes and roll them up. Put the crêpes side by side in a shallow heatproof dish then sprinkle over the Parmesan cheese.
5. Put the crêpes under a hot grill for a few minutes until the cheese has melted and everything is bubbling hot. Serve at once.

SERVES 4

VARIATION

CHILLI CREPES

These are nice served with some guacamole and soured cream, or a chopped avocado salad. Increase the amount of tomatoes to 450g/1lb and use a 425g/15oz can of red kidney beans, drained, instead of the courgettes. Cook as above, seasoning the mixture with a good pinch of chilli powder. Substitute Cheddar cheese for the Parmesan.

CHOCOLATE AND CHERRY CREPES

These are best made with fresh, ripe black cherries, which you need to stone. Wear rubber gloves so your nails don't get stained and use a cherry stoner or a sharp knife.

450g / 1lb ripe black   chocolate crêpe batter
  cherries   (see page 38)
caster sugar   150ml / 5fl oz soured
dash of kirsch   cream

1. Stone the cherries then put them into a bowl and sprinkle with a little sugar and a dash of kirsch.
2. Make the crêpes as described on page 38.
3. Spread the crêpes with the soured cream and top with the cherries. Roll them up, sprinkle with sugar and serve.
SERVES 4

CREPES SUZETTE WITH MIXED BERRIES

These are wonderful for a quick special pudding but I also like them as an unconventional light meal.

orange crêpe batter   4 tbls orange-
  (see page 38)   flavoured liqueur
125g / 4oz unsalted   such as Cointreau or
  butter   Grand Marnier, or
150ml / 5fl oz freshly   brandy
  squeezed orange juice 50g / 2oz redcurrants
grated rind of 1 orange   and blueberries
125g / 4oz caster sugar

1. Make the crêpes as described on page 38, using melted butter to grease the frying pan.
2. Gently melt the unsalted butter in a large frying pan then add the orange juice and rind, sugar and half the liqueur or brandy. Heat this mixture gently.

3. Place one crêpe in the pan and cook for a few seconds to heat it through. Fold it in half then in half again to make a triangle and push it to the far side of the pan. Repeat this process with the remaining crêpes. Sprinkle the redcurrants and blueberries into the pan.
4. Put the remaining liqueur or brandy into a metal ladle or a small saucepan and warm it over the gas flame or hot plate. When it is tepid, set it alight with a match, standing well back and averting your face. Pour it over the crêpes and serve immediately.
SERVES 4

APPLE CREPES

Although sweet crêpes are usually served as a pudding, I rather like to have them occasionally as a light main course, instead of at the end of a meal when I feel too full to enjoy them. A pudding and a pot of black coffee make a pleasant meal occasionally!

orange crêpe batter   2–3 tsp granulated
  (see page 38)   sugar
450g / 1lb sweet,   50g / 2oz sultanas or
  mellow eating apples   raisins (optional)
  such as Cox's   a little caster sugar
15g / ½oz butter

1. Make the crêpes as described on page 38.
2. Peel and core the apples and slice them thinly. Melt the butter in a saucepan, add the apples and sugar, and the sultanas or raisins if you are using them, and stir to mix together. Cook, uncovered, over a low heat, stirring gently from time to time, for about 3–4 minutes or until the apples slices have softened.
3. Spoon this mixture on to the crêpes and roll them up. Sprinkle with a little caster sugar and serve immediately, perhaps with some crème fraîche.
SERVES 4

These crêpes are particularly delicious if you add to the apple mixture a good pinch of cinnamon and/or ground cloves or a splash of Calvados.

CHEESE SALADS

—— ✳ ——

ROQUEFORT SALAD

1 oak-leaf lettuce
1 tbls rice vinegar
1 tbls olive oil
salt and freshly
  ground black pepper
1–2 tbls chopped fresh
  chives
100g / 3½ oz Roquefort
  cheese

1　Wash the lettuce and put the leaves in a salad spinner or colander to drain.

2　Put the rice vinegar, oil and some seasoning into a salad bowl and mix. Then put in the chives. Tear the lettuce roughly on top.

3　Cut or break the Roquefort into pieces and add to the bowl, then gently toss the salad to coat the leaves with dressing and distribute the ingredients.
SERVES 2

——  ——

BROCCOLI, CHERRY TOMATO AND FETA SALAD

1 tbls olive oil
1 tbls rice vinegar
salt and freshly
  ground black pepper
225g / 8oz cherry
  tomatoes
4 spring onions
100g / 3½ oz feta cheese
450g / 1lb broccoli
a few sprigs of
  oregano

1　Put the oil, vinegar and some seasoning into a salad bowl. Halve the tomatoes, trim and chop the spring onions and put them in the bowl. Break the feta into rough chunks and add to the bowl, too.

OPPOSITE: *(left) Broccoli, Cherry Tomato and Feta Salad, (top) Warm Carrot and Goat's Cheese Salad, (right) Roquefort Salad*

2　Wash the broccoli and separate it into small florets. Peel and slice the stems. Cook, covered, in 2.5 cm/1 inch of boiling water for 4 minutes, then drain immediately into a sieve, pat dry with kitchen paper and add to the other ingredients in the bowl.

3　Tear the oregano over the top, mix gently and serve the salad at once, while it is still warm.
SERVES 2

—— ——

WARM CARROT AND GOAT'S CHEESE SALAD

The idea for this came from an excellent quiche I ate at Stephen Bull's restaurant in London. I loved the combination of ingredients, which I have recreated as this salad, adding a thyme and honey vinaigrette.

200g / 7oz firm goat's
  cheese log
8 sun-dried tomatoes
  in oil, drained
450g / 1lb carrots
2 tbls oil from the sun-
  dried tomatoes
4 tsp clear honey
2 tbls balsamic
  vinegar
½ tsp dried thyme or
  1 tsp chopped fresh
  thyme
salt and freshly
  ground black pepper
sprigs of fresh thyme

1　Cut the goat's cheese into 6 mm/¼ inch dice and put it into a bowl. Chop the sun-dried tomatoes and add these to the bowl, too.

2　Scrape the carrots and slice them very thinly – the side of a grater or a mandolin is good for this. Cook in a little boiling water for 1 minute; drain, pat dry with kitchen paper and add to the bowl.

3　Add the oil, honey, vinegar, thyme, a little salt and a grinding or two of pepper and mix well. Garnish with the sprigs of thyme then serve at once, while the carrots are still warm.
SERVES 2–4

I like rice vinegar because it's light and sweet, so you can use less oil in the dressing and thus reduce the dreaded calories.

CHEESE DIP WITH CRUDITES

In my experience this is very popular with children and teenagers – and a good way of encouraging them to eat more vegetables, since they can choose their favourite raw vegetables and salad ingredients to eat with it.

about 350g / 12oz raw vegetables: sticks of cucumber, carrot and celery; small florets of cauliflower; cherry tomatoes, radishes, spring onions; crisp lettuce, etc.
50g / 2oz Cheddar or other hard cheese

25g / 1oz low-fat soft cheese or plain yogurt, or 2 tbls milk and 15g / ½ oz soft butter
freshly ground black pepper

1 Prepare the vegetables, cutting them into pieces suitable for dipping.

2 Finely grate the cheese. Put it into a bowl with the soft cheese, yogurt, or milk and butter and beat them together until creamy.

3 Season with pepper, then spoon into a small dish and put this on a plate or into a shallow basket, surrounded by the vegetables. Or you can spoon the dip straight on to a plate and arrange the vegetables around it.

SERVES 1

A REALLY GOOD PLOUGHMAN'S

A ploughman's lunch can be delicious, although in my experience the ones you get in pubs often aren't: hunks of boring bread and cheese, syrupy brown pickle, some tired lettuce and tomato, and a spoonful of synthetic-tasting coleslaw. But choose the cheese with care and serve it with good, warm bread, fresh, crisp salad and interesting pickles, and it's a feast.

fresh, crusty bread, white, wholewheat or granary
butter (optional)
50–100g / 2–3½oz mature farmhouse Cheddar or Stilton cheese

crisp lettuce leaves
1 firm tomato, sliced
pickled onions or other pickle to taste

1 Warm the bread, then cut or break it into thick slices and arrange it on a platter with the remaining ingredients. Serve with a glass of beer or cider.

SERVES 1

VARIATIONS

1 FRENCH PLOUGHMAN'S

Use good crusty French bread – either a baguette or French country bread – and a French cheese of your choice: Brie or a firm goat's cheese would be fine. Add a handful of black olives, some salad leaves such as lamb's lettuce or chicory, and plum tomatoes. Serve with French red country wine.

2 GREEK PLOUGHMAN'S

The basis of this variation is some crumbly, salty feta cheese and some Kalamata olives. Serve with soft, country-style bread and a tomato and onion salad, and drink some chilled white wine with it.

3 GERMAN PLOUGHMAN'S

Choose a dark rye bread, such as pumpernickel, and cheese flavoured with caraway or cumin seeds or paprika. Serve with pickled cucumbers.

GRILLED GOAT'S CHEESE SALAD

In fashionable circles this is now regarded as a bit of a has-been, but really it's a classic and so quick, as well as being one of my personal favourites. It's best if the goat's cheese log is the same width as the baguette.

125g / 4oz mixed salad leaves	125g / 4oz goat's cheese log
fresh herbs, if available; chervil is especially good	1 tsp balsamic vinegar
	1 tbls olive oil
2–4 thin slices of baguette	salt and freshly ground black pepper

1 Wash the salad leaves, shake them dry and put them into a bowl with some torn-up herbs, if you have them.

2 Lightly toast the baguette slices on one side under the grill.

3 Cut the goat's cheese into 2 or 4 slices and place on the untoasted side of the baguette, then put them under the grill until brown and bubbling.

4 Meanwhile, sprinkle the vinegar and oil over the salad with a little salt and pepper and toss the leaves. Cut the pieces of baguette in half, put them on top of the salad, and serve at once.

SERVES 1

NO-COOK CHEESE FEASTS

With the excellent cheeses, breads, fruit and vegetables that are now widely available, you can put together a wonderful feast that requires no cooking and hardly any preparation – just a bit of careful shopping. Here are some good combinations: you could serve one or several at a time, depending on the number of people. Some red or white wine (or fruit juice spritzers) would complete the spread. You need to allow about 125g/4oz cheese per person.

1 APPLES AND CHEDDAR

Choose really good apples with melting, sweet flesh – mature Cox's or Russets, for instance – and a good, mature farmhouse Cheddar. Some whole-wheat bread, especially the home-made, rather heavy, moist type, goes well with this.

2 VIGNOTTE OR CAMEMBERT AND GRAPES

This is a gorgeous combination, more like a pudding than a main course. Choose the best grapes available – perhaps a mixture of two colours – and some crumbly oatcakes.

3 PEAR WITH GORGONZOLA OR PECORINO

Buttery, sweet ripe pears – preferably Comice – with either Gorgonzola or Pecorino cheese, and perhaps some peppery watercress or rocket leaves and good plain Italian bread.

4 RICOTTA, BLUE CHEESE AND CELERY

Two contrasting cheeses and crisp, clean-tasting celery stalks make a good combination. Serve either warm, crusty bread or some thin crackers to accompany them.

5 INSALATA TRICOLORE

Slice some good-quality, water-packed Mozzarella cheese – preferably buffalo Mozzarella – and arrange it on a plate with sliced plum or beefsteak tomatoes, slices of ripe avocado tossed in lemon juice, and torn leaves of fresh basil. Serve this classic salad with warm Italian bread.

6 CREAM CHEESE WITH RIPE PINEAPPLE

The success of this depends more than anything on the quality of the pineapple. If you can get a really ripe, sweet, juicy one, it can be superb. Peel the pineapple, removing all the little tufts and the inner core, then cut it into chunks or slices and arrange on a plate with the cheese. You could use mascarpone or a cream cheese from the deli: both full-fat and lighter varieties are fine.

For an even quicker cheese salad that never seems to go out of fashion, mash 50g / 2 oz blue cheese with 4 tablespoons of yogurt or soured cream, season to taste then spoon on top of little gem lettuces, cut into quarters.

Pineapples are usually ready to eat when they smell slightly syrupy and one of the inner leaves pulls out easily.

FRIED, MELTED & GRILLED CHEESE

✳

HALOUMI WITH SPICED LEEKS

Moist, tender leeks spiced up with cumin seed and the sharp tang of lime make a delicious base for crisp slices of haloumi cheese. Serve this with a salad, bread or rice. Basmati rice will cook quickly while you're preparing the haloumi mixture.

Haloumi is an unusual cheese because it is very firm and keeps its shape well when grilled or fried. Read the packet to make sure you're getting a vegetarian one. Unopened, it keeps for ages in the fridge and for even longer in the freezer.

700g / 1½ lb tender
  leeks, trimmed to
  give 450g / 1lb
225g / 8oz haloumi
  cheese

2 tbls olive oil
½ tsp cumin seeds
juice of 1 lime
salt and freshly
  ground black pepper

1 Slice the leeks fairly finely. Cut the cheese into slices about 8 mm/⅓ inch thick then cut each slice in half to make squarish pieces.

2 Heat the oil in a frying pan, put in the cheese and fry for 1–2 minutes until golden brown on one side, then flip the pieces over and fry the other side. This whole process only takes 2–3 minutes.

3 Drain the cheese on kitchen paper and leave on one side.

4 Put the leeks into the frying pan and stir-fry for about 5 minutes or until they are just tender. Then add the cumin seeds and stir for a moment or two longer. Add the lime juice and season with salt and pepper.

5 Put the cheese back into the pan with the leeks and heat through for a few minutes. Serve on warm plates.
SERVES 2

HALOUMI AND COURGETTES WITH TOMATO SALSA

225g / 8oz tomatoes
½ onion, peeled and
  chopped
2 tbls chopped fresh
  coriander
salt and freshly
  ground black pepper

350g / 12oz courgettes
225g / 8oz haloumi
  cheese
3 tbls olive oil

1 First make the salsa: pour boiling water over the tomatoes, leave for a few seconds, then drain and cover with cold water. Slip off the skins with a sharp knife then chop the tomatoes and put them into a bowl. Add the onion, coriander and some salt and pepper to taste.

2 Wash and thinly slice the courgettes. Cut the cheese into slices about 8 mm/⅓ inch thick then cut each slice in half to make squarish pieces.

3 Heat 2 tablespoons of the oil in a frying pan, put in the courgettes and fry for 3–4 minutes or until they are tender and golden brown in patches. Then remove them from the pan and keep them warm.

4 Heat the remaining oil in the pan, put in the cheese and fry for 1–2 minutes, until it is golden brown on one side. Then flip the pieces over and fry the other side. This whole process only takes 2–3 minutes.

5 Put the courgettes back in the pan, mix with the haloumi and turn gently to make sure everything is really hot. Serve on to plates and top with the salsa.
SERVES 2

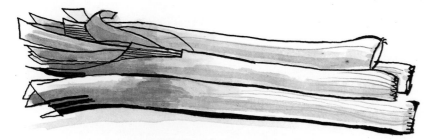

OPPOSITE: *Haloumi with Spiced Leeks*

DEEP-FRIED CAMEMBERT

If you're just making this for one or two people the cheese can be fried in a medium saucepan in a relatively small amount of oil, saving the hassle of using a deep-fryer. Serve on top of some green salad leaves, if you like; the combination of hot, melted cheese and cool, crisp leaves is particularly good. I like some sweet mango chutney or apricot jam with it, too.

You can vary the fondue by using different cheeses: try Cheddar and light ale for a very British flavour, or blue cheese with cider or a fruity white wine.

1 box of Camembert cheese triangles, chilled in the fridge
1 egg, beaten with 1 tbls water
dried breadcrumbs for coating
oil for deep-frying

1 Dip the pieces of Camembert into the beaten egg, then into the crumbs to coat them. Repeat the process so that they are really well coated then chill them in the fridge while you heat the oil.

2 Half-fill a saucepan with oil and heat it. Test the temperature by dipping a wooden chopstick or the handle of a wooden spoon into it: the oil should immediately form bubbles around it.

3 Put in the pieces of Camembert and fry for 4–5 minutes, until they are crisp and golden brown. Remove them with a draining spoon and put them on crumpled kitchen paper to absorb excess oil. Serve immediately.

SERVES 2

CHEESE FONDUE

Cheese fondue is very quick to make. It can be served from the pan without using a fondue burner, or simply poured over crusty warm bread, though I think it's more fun to eat if you dip the bread into it. You can make fondue for one person but it's more enjoyable when you're sharing it.

1 French stick
1 garlic clove, halved
225g / 8oz Edam or Emmenthal cheese
150ml / 5fl oz dry white wine or cider
2 tsp cornflour
1 tsp lemon juice
salt and freshly ground black pepper
freshly grated nutmeg

1 Cut or break the bread into bite-sized pieces, spread them out on a baking sheet or heatproof dish and put them under a not-too-hot grill to warm.

2 Rub the garlic around the inside of a medium-sized saucepan, then discard it. Grate the cheese.

3 Put all but 1 tablespoon of the wine or cider into the saucepan, add the cheese and bring just to the boil – the cheese will look like a lumpy mess at this stage but don't worry.

4 Blend the cornflour with the remaining wine or cider then pour this into the cheese mixture, stirring vigorously over the heat. The mixture will thicken and become smooth.

5 Remove from the heat and add the lemon juice and some salt, pepper and grated nutmeg to taste. Serve at once with the warm bread, and have long forks available so that you can spear pieces of bread and dip them into the fondue in the pan.

SERVES 2

GRILLED BRIE WITH ALMONDS

This is very easy and makes a good quick meal served with a crisp leafy salad or a tomato salad.

225–350g / 8–12oz Brie
25g / 1oz flaked
  almonds

[1] Slice the Brie, including the rind, and arrange it in a shallow layer in a heatproof dish.
[2] Place the dish under a hot grill for about 5–7 minutes, until the Brie has begun to melt, then sprinkle the almonds evenly on top and grill for a few more minutes, until the nuts have toasted. Watch it carefully because they will burn quickly. Serve at once.
SERVES 2

GRILLED FETA WITH OLIVES

This quick supper dish needs to be served with plenty of soft, plain bread – no butter – and some salad leaves.

225g / 8oz feta cheese   **50g / 2oz large green**
50g / 2oz black olives,   **olives**
  preferably Kalamata

[1] Heat the grill. Cut the feta cheese into cubes and put them into a shallow heatproof dish. Add the olives, distributing them amongst the cheese.
[2] Heat under the grill for about 5 minutes, or until the feta is melting and has become golden brown in places. Serve at once.
SERVES 2

CHEESY TOMATO GRILL

A good recipe for when you're on a diet or watching your fat intake. You can leave the Parmesan out if you want to reduce the fat and calories even further, but it is only a very small amount and it does add a lot of flavour. Peppery salad ingredients such as watercress or rocket go well with this, or some quickly steamed broccoli or French beans.

1 beefsteak tomato   **15g / ½ oz fresh**
salt and freshly   **Parmesan cheese, cut**
  ground black pepper   **into slivers or grated**
a few fresh basil
  leaves
125g / 4oz very-low-
  fat cottage cheese,
  plain or with chives
  and/or onion

[1] Heat the grill. Slice the tomato into thick rounds. Place these in a shallow ovenproof dish in a single layer, season with salt and pepper and tear over some basil leaves.
[2] Spoon the cottage cheese evenly over the tomato, then sprinkle with the Parmesan cheese.
[3] Grill for about 10 minutes, or until everything is heated through and the top is golden brown.
SERVES 1

PUDDINGS WITH CHEESE, CREAM & YOGURT

✳

This is a very quick chocolate pudding, consisting of a biscuity base with a light, creamy chocolate topping. You can eat it almost immediately or leave it overnight – it just gets better all the time! It's a useful emergency pudding because the ingredients are so simple, but it is essential that you use good-quality plain chocolate.

CHOCOLATE AMARETTI PUDDING

300g / 10oz plain chocolate, at least 50% cocoa solids
25g / 1oz butter
125g / 4oz amaretti biscuits

200ml / 7fl oz single cream
½ tsp finely grated orange rind
strands of orange rind to decorate

1 First make a start on the topping: break 200g/7oz of the chocolate into pieces and put them into a deep bowl set over a pan of steaming water. Leave until the chocolate has melted then remove the bowl from the pan and stand it in a bowl of cold water to cool it down quickly.

2 While the chocolate is melting, make the base, but first draw a potato peeler down the length of the remaining chocolate to make a few chocolate curls for decorating the pudding: keep these on one side. Break the rest of the chocolate into pieces, put them into a medium saucepan with the butter and melt over a very low heat.

3 Crush the amaretti biscuits then remove the chocolate mixture from the heat and stir in the biscuit crumbs until they are well coated.

4 Put a 17.5–20 cm/7–8 inch plain flan ring on a plate and spoon the crumb mixture into it, pressing it down firmly with the back of a spoon. Put it in a cool place (I put mine in the freezer).

5 Now pour the cream into the bowl of melted chocolate, add the grated orange rind and whisk until thick and pale. This will only take a few minutes if the mixture is cold enough: if it takes longer, put it in the fridge or freezer for a few minutes.

6 Spoon the chocolate cream on to the base, taking it right to the edges and smoothing the top with the back of the spoon. You can serve it almost immediately or refrigerate it. Run a knife around the edges and remove the flan ring, neatening the

edges with the knife – the longer you leave it the easier it will be to turn out. Decorate the top with the reserved chocolate curls and the orange strands before serving. It's nice as it is, or with some extra single cream, or with cream lightly whipped with 1 tablespoon of rum, brandy or Amaretto liqueur.
SERVES 4–6

GREEK YOGURT WITH FRESH DATES

This is my slightly adapted version of one of Prue Leith's ideas. As she says, the better the quality of the ingredients you use, the better the pudding will be.

50g / 2oz almonds
225g / 8oz fresh dates
450g / 1lb thick Greek yogurt

4 tbls thick cream
4 tbls clear honey such as acacia

1 First skin the almonds: put them into a small saucepan, cover with water and boil for 1 minute. Then remove from the heat, drain, and pop the nuts out of their skins. Chop them roughly.

2 Stone the dates and chop them roughly.

3 Put a few dates in the bottom of four glass bowls. Put 2 good heaped tablespoons of yogurt into each bowl then put the rest of the dates on top. Spoon the cream on top, then drizzle the honey over that and finally sprinkle over the chopped almonds.
SERVES 4

OPPOSITE: *(left) Chocolate Amaretti Pudding, (centre) Ricotta Cream with Crystallized Fruit, page 52, (right) Greek Yogurt with Fresh Dates*

RICOTTA CREAM WITH CRYSTALLIZED FRUIT

This is a nice pudding to make when there is some colourful crystallized fruit available. Vanilla sugar is easy to make, but if you haven't got any, use ordinary caster sugar and a few drops of real vanilla extract.

175g / 6oz mixed
  crystallized fruit
2 tbls Marsala wine
50g / 2oz almonds

175g / 6oz ricotta
  cheese
1 tbls single cream
1 tbls vanilla sugar

1 Cut the crystallized fruit into fairly small pieces. Put them into a bowl and add the Marsala.
2 Put the almonds into a small saucepan, cover with water and boil for 1 minute. Then remove from the heat, drain, and pop the nuts out of their skins. Stir them into the fruit mixture.
3 Put the ricotta into a bowl and mix in the cream and vanilla sugar. Leave in a cool place until you want to serve the pudding. Stir the fruit again.
4 To serve, divide the ricotta mixture between two plates then spoon the fruit on to the plates.
SERVES 2

MASCARPONE LEMON CREAM

The lemon cuts the richness of the mascarpone in this delectable and easy pudding.

225g / 8oz mascarpone
  cheese
rind and juice of
  ½ lemon

25–50g / 1–2oz sugar
slivers of lemon rind
  to decorate

1 Put the mascarpone cheese into a bowl with the lemon rind and juice and mix until smooth.
2 Mix in sugar to taste then spoon into dishes and decorate with slivers of lemon rind.
SERVES 2–3

A zester, which is inexpensive to buy, is invaluable for producing long strands of citrus rind quickly and easily.

COFFEE RICOTTA PUDDING

Ricotta is a medium-fat cheese, so this isn't very calorific; you could make it even less so by using a low-fat soft cheese, if you wish. A really good-quality instant espresso coffee will give this the best flavour.

225g / 8oz ricotta
  cheese
1 tsp instant espresso
  coffee
25–50g / 1–2oz sugar

chocolate-covered
  coffee beans, flakes of
  chocolate or toasted
  flaked almonds to
  decorate

1 Put the ricotta cheese into a bowl and break it up with a spoon.
2 Dissolve the coffee in 1 tablespoon of hot water and add it to the ricotta, then add sugar to taste.
3 Mix until everything is well blended, then spoon into individual dishes and decorate with chocolate-covered coffee beans, a few flakes of chocolate or some toasted flaked almonds.
SERVES 2

YOGURT BRULEE

This can be as rich or as low in fat as you wish, depending on the type of yogurt you use and whether you add any cream. In any case, the crisp topping, which you have to smash with your spoon before eating the yogurt, makes it special.

300ml / ½ pint plain
  yogurt, or 150ml / 5fl
  oz plain yogurt and
  150ml / 5fl oz double
  or whipping cream

75g / 3oz caster sugar,
  plus extra to sweeten
  if desired

1 If you are using cream, whisk this until thick then fold in the yogurt. Sweeten to taste with a little sugar if you wish, remembering that the topping will add sweetness.

2 Spoon the yogurt or yogurt and cream into two ramekins, leaving some space at the top.

3 Put the caster sugar into a small saucepan and heat gently until it has turned to syrup and become golden brown – don't let it get too dark. Then immediately pour it over the yogurt. It will set hard within a few minutes; chill until needed.

SERVES 2

LIME CHEESECAKE

This is astonishingly quick to make, though it won't come to any harm if you keep it, well covered, in the fridge for several hours or even overnight. Some single cream and/or fresh fruit go well with it.

50g / 2oz butter	*50g / 2oz caster sugar*
175g / 6oz digestive biscuits	*150ml / 5fl oz double cream*
225g / 8oz low-fat soft white cheese	*thin slices of lime or slivers of rind and a*
grated rind and juice of ½ lime	*few crushed pistachio nuts to decorate*

1 First make the cheesecake base: melt the butter in a saucepan over a gentle heat; crush the biscuits into crumbs. Stir the biscuit crumbs into the butter, off the heat, until they are well coated.

2 Put a 20 cm/8 inch plain flan ring on a plate and spoon in the crumbs, pressing down with the back of the spoon. Put it in a cold place while you make the topping (I put mine in the freezer).

3 Put the soft cheese into a bowl with the lime rind and juice, sugar and double cream. Stir vigorously for 1–2 minutes, until very thick.

4 Spoon the filling on top of the base, taking it right to the edges. Decorate with lime slices or rind and pistachio nuts. You can serve it almost immediately, as it sets quickly, or leave it in the fridge. Run a knife around the edges and remove the flan ring, neatening the edges with the knife.

SERVES 4

QUICK CHOCOLATE WHIP

This can be whipped together in a few minutes and is a real treat, served in small glasses with some light, crisp biscuits.

300g / 10oz plain chocolate, at least 50% cocoa solids	*flakes of plain chocolate*
300 ml / ½ pint single cream	

1 Break the chocolate into pieces and put it into a deep bowl set over a pan of steaming water. Leave until the chocolate has melted then remove the bowl from the pan and put it in a cool place or in a bowl of cold water to cool it down quickly.

2 When the chocolate has cooled a little, pour in the single cream, which will cool it down further. Then whisk until the mixture gets thick and pale. This will only take a few minutes if the mixture is cold enough; if it takes longer, put it in the fridge or freezer for a few minutes.

3 Spoon the thick chocolate whip into glasses, decorate with the chocolate flakes and keep in the fridge or a cool place until required.

SERVES 4

VARIATION

1 RUM AND RAISIN CHOCOLATE WHIP

Before you start making the whip, put 50g/2 oz raisins into a small bowl, cover with 2 tablespoons of rum and leave to plump up. Divide the raisins and any liquid that hasn't been absorbed between 4 glasses, then spoon the chocolate mixture on top.

To clean a pan in which sugar syrup has been made, leave the pan to cool then fill it with water and bring to the boil: this will dissolve the hard, sticky coating, making the pan easy to clean.

To crush biscuits, put them into a large polythene bag and roll with a rolling pin.

PASTA

As long as you have a packet of pasta in the cupboard you can always rustle up a quick meal: pasta is good even when served simply with just olive oil or butter. If you add a few more ingredients and make sure you have plenty of different pasta shapes in your storecupboard, the scope is enormous. Dishes such as Quick Mediterranean Pasta, Fusilli with Fennel and Mangetout, Spinach Tagliatelle with Walnuts and Fettuccine with Asparagus Sauce can all be made within 30 minutes, and they need little accompaniment – perhaps a simple salad or some bread – to make a satisfying meal.

TOMATO SAUCES
✳

QUICK MEDITERRANEAN PASTA

I like this with some full-bodied red wine and a leafy salad containing rocket – some supermarket salad mixes include it. Dress the salad with 2 teaspoons of red wine vinegar, 2 tablespoons of olive oil and some seasoning, and serve with the pasta.

1 tbls oil from the
  sun-dried tomatoes
1 onion, peeled and
  chopped
2 garlic cloves, crushed
1 × 400g / 14oz can
  tomatoes
8 sun-dried tomatoes
  in oil, drained
½ × 400g / 14oz can
  artichoke hearts

50g / 2oz black olives
salt and freshly
  ground black pepper
225g / 8oz penne rigate
  or rigatoni
6 fresh basil leaves
fresh Parmesan cheese,
  cut into slivers
  (optional)

1 First fill a saucepan with 2 litres/3½ pints of water and bring to the boil for the pasta.

2 Meanwhile, heat the oil in a saucepan then add the onion, cover and cook gently for 10 minutes, until tender but not brown. Stir in the garlic and cook for 1–2 minutes longer.

3 Add the tomatoes, together with their juice, breaking them up with a wooden spoon. Chop the sun-dried tomatoes and add these to the pan too. Simmer for about 10–15 minutes, until the liquid has evaporated. Meanwhile, drain and slice the artichoke hearts and add these to the sauce along with the olives and plenty of salt and pepper.

4 When the water boils, add the pasta and let it bubble away, uncovered, for about 8 minutes or until it is *al dente*. Drain the pasta, return it to the pan and season with some salt; then add the sauce and stir so that all the pasta gets coated.

5 Tear the basil over the pasta, then serve topped with slivers of Parmesan cheese, if you like.
SERVES 2

SPAGHETTI WITH ROASTED PEPPER AND TOMATO SAUCE

Roasted red pepper and sun-dried tomatoes give this a mellow, slightly sweet flavour; a leafy salad and some shavings of fresh Parmesan go perfectly with it.

1 red pepper
225g / 8oz spaghetti
1 onion, peeled and
  chopped
1 tbls oil from the
  sun-dried tomatoes
1–2 garlic cloves,
  crushed

1 × 400g / 14oz can
  tomatoes
4 sun-dried tomatoes
  in oil, drained
salt and freshly
  ground black pepper
fresh Parmesan cheese,
  cut into slivers

1 Cut the pepper into quarters, put it on a grill pan cut-side down and grill under a high heat for about 10 minutes, until charred and blistered in places. Remove from the heat, cool slightly then peel off the skin and discard the stem and seeds.

2 Fill a saucepan with 2 litres/3½ pints of water and bring to the boil, then add the spaghetti and cook, uncovered, for about 8 minutes, until *al dente*.

3 Meanwhile, cook the onion gently in the oil for 10 minutes, until tender but not brown. Add the garlic and cook for 1–2 minutes longer, then stir in the canned tomatoes and their juice, breaking them up with a wooden spoon. Chop the sun-dried tomatoes and add these to the pan too. Simmer for about 10–15 minutes, until the liquid has evaporated.

4 Either put the sauce into a food processor with the red pepper and whizz to a purée, or chop the pepper and stir it into the sauce. Season well. Drain the pasta, return it to the saucepan and add some salt, then stir in the sauce so that all the pasta gets coated. Serve topped with slivers of Parmesan.
SERVES 2

OPPOSITE: *Quick Mediterranean Pasta*

PENNE WITH CHILLI, TOMATO AND MUSHROOM SAUCE

The chilli gives this sauce a kick while a splash of cream cools it down a bit, making a nice balance – though you could leave out either of them and the sauce would still be good.

225g / 8oz button
  mushrooms
1 green chilli
1 tbls oil
1 onion, peeled and
  chopped
1 garlic clove, crushed
1 × 400g / 14oz can
  tomatoes

225g / 8oz penne
4 tbls cream
salt and freshly
  ground black pepper
fresh Parmesan cheese,
  grated

Some supermarkets now sell tomatoes that are 'grown for flavour' – why can't this apply to them all? – and these are worth trying. Shiny red plum tomatoes are usually a good bet too.

1. First fill a saucepan with 2 litres/3½ pints of water and bring to the boil for the pasta.
2. Meanwhile, slice the mushrooms and halve, de-seed and chop the chilli. Fry them in the oil in a large saucepan, along with the onion and garlic, for about 10 minutes, until softened but not brown.
3. Stir in the tomatoes and their juice, breaking them up with a wooden spoon, then simmer for 10–15 minutes, until the liquid has evaporated.
4. When the water boils, add the pasta and let it bubble away, uncovered, for about 8 minutes or until it is *al dente*. Meanwhile, stir the cream into the sauce and season it with salt and pepper.
5. Drain the pasta, return it to the still-warm saucepan and season with some salt. Then add the sauce and stir so that all the pasta gets coated. Serve out on to warm plates and hand round fresh Parmesan cheese separately.

SERVES 2

VARIATION

PENNE WITH PIQUANT SAUCE

This is a lively dish, particularly good on a chilly night. Cook the pasta and make the tomato sauce as above, but omit the mushrooms, chilli and cream. Instead, when the sauce is cooked, add 50g/2oz black olives, stoned and chopped, 1 tablespoon of capers, and a good pinch each of chilli powder and cayenne pepper. Season with salt and pepper and add more chilli or cayenne, if necessary. Serve with grated Parmesan.

FETTUCCINE WITH FRESH TOMATO SAUCE

This is at its best in the summer when made from flavourful fresh tomatoes.

1 tbls olive oil
1 onion, peeled and
  chopped
450g / 1lb fresh
  tomatoes
1 garlic clove, crushed
225g / 8oz fettuccine or
  other delicate pasta

salt and freshly
  ground black pepper
6–8 fresh basil leaves
fresh Parmesan cheese,
  grated (optional)

1. First fill a saucepan with 2 litres/3½ pints of water and bring to the boil for the pasta.
2. Next start making the sauce: heat the oil in a large saucepan then add the onion, cover and cook gently for 10 minutes, until tender but not brown.
3. Meanwhile, put the tomatoes in a bowl, cover with boiling water and leave for a few seconds until the skins loosen. Drain, cover with cold water and slip off the skins. Chop the tomatoes roughly, removing any hard bits of core.
4. Stir the garlic into the onion and cook for 1–2 minutes longer, then stir in the tomatoes and leave to cook, uncovered, for about 10–15 minutes, until the sauce is thick with no trace of wateriness.
5. When the water boils, add the fettuccine and let it bubble away, uncovered, for about 8 minutes or until it is *al dente*. Drain the pasta, return it to the pan and add the sauce. Season very well then mix together and tear the basil leaves over. Serve at once, with fresh Parmesan cheese if you like.

SERVES 2

LIGHT PASTA DISHES

---✳---

PENNE WITH GRILLED PEPPERS AND ROCKET

Grilled peppers, so moist and tender and sweet, make an excellent contrast to firm pasta, and the peppery rocket adds the final touch. If you can't get rocket, use some fresh basil leaves instead but add them straight to the cooked pasta; don't wilt them in the hot oil first.

1 large red pepper	*salt and freshly*
1 large yellow pepper	*ground black pepper*
small handful of	*1 garlic clove, crushed*
rocket	*fresh Parmesan cheese,*
175g / 6oz penne, or	*cut into slivers*
similar-shaped pasta	*(optional)*
2 tbls olive oil	

1. First prepare the peppers: cut them into quarters, put them on a grill pan cut-side down and grill under a high heat until the skin has charred and blistered in places – this will take about 10 minutes and the pieces may need turning to make sure they grill evenly. When they are done, remove them from the heat and cover with a damp tea towel to cool them down and help loosen the skin.
2. Next fill a saucepan with 2 litres/3½ pints of water and bring to the boil for the pasta.
3. Wash the rocket but don't chop it. Strip the skin off the peppers with a sharp knife, discard the stems and seeds and cut the flesh into long, thin pieces.
4. When the water boils, add the pasta to the pan then let it bubble away, uncovered, for about 8 minutes or until it is *al dente*. Drain the pasta, return it to the still-warm saucepan and gently mix in 1 tablespoon of the oil and some salt to taste. Cover and keep warm.
5. Heat the remaining oil in another pan and put in the garlic, rocket and peppers; stir-fry for 1–2 minutes until everything is heated through, then tip the whole lot in with the pasta and toss well to combine. Check the seasoning and add some coarsely ground black pepper, then serve out on to warm plates and top with some slivers of Parmesan cheese if you wish.
SERVES 2

PASTA WITH PESTO

Pasta with pesto is delicious, and very quick to prepare using ready-made pesto. However, if you have a food processor you can easily whizz up your own. I like to use a long pasta such as spaghetti or tagliatelle and to serve it with a simple tomato and lettuce salad with a vinaigrette dressing.

225g / 8oz pasta	*4 tbls olive oil*
50g / 2oz fresh basil	*salt and freshly*
25g / 1oz fresh	*ground black pepper*
Parmesan cheese,	*fresh Parmesan cheese,*
grated	*grated, to serve*
25g / 1oz pine nuts	

1. Fill a saucepan with 2 litres/3½ pints of water and put it on the stove to heat up for the pasta. When the water boils, add the pasta to the pan then let it bubble away, uncovered, for about 8 minutes or until it is *al dente*.
2. While the pasta is cooking, make the pesto: wash the basil and remove any large stems then put the leaves into a food processor or liquidizer along with the grated Parmesan cheese, pine nuts and olive oil. Whizz together briefly to make a bright green sauce.
3. Drain the pasta then put it back into the still-warm pan. Add the pesto, season well, then serve out on to warmed plates and hand round extra Parmesan cheese.
SERVES 2

PAPPARDELLE WITH PORCINI

Pappardelle is a particularly satisfying pasta – thick ribbons that you can really get your teeth into – and in this recipe it picks up the delicious flavour of the porcini mushrooms. Some extra shavings of fresh Parmesan make a nice finishing touch.

Dried porcini mushrooms – or ceps if you get the French ones – can be bought in tiny packets and are now stocked by some large supermarkets. They can be used on their own or added to mushroom mixtures to intensify the flavour.

1 × 10–15g / ¼–½oz packet of dried porcini mushrooms	salt and freshly ground black pepper
225g / 8oz pappardelle	fresh Parmesan cheese, cut into slivers
25g / 1oz butter	

1 Put the porcini into a small bowl and cover with boiling water. Leave on one side to soak.

2 Next fill a saucepan with 2 litres/3½ pints of water and bring it to the boil. Add the pasta to the pan, then let it bubble away, uncovered, for about 8 minutes or until it is *al dente*.

3 Just before the pasta is ready, drain the porcini through a sieve lined with a piece of kitchen paper or muslin and placed over a bowl. Chop the porcini finely, then put them into a small saucepan with their soaking liquid and boil for a few minutes until almost all the liquid has gone.

4 Drain the pasta then put it back into the still-warm pan with the butter, the porcini and some salt and pepper to taste. Mix gently, then serve out on to warmed plates and top with slivers of fresh Parmesan cheese.

SERVES 2

PASTA WITH FRESH HERBS

There are some excitingly flavoured pastas around and these are fun to try for a change, although I must say they often look much more exotic than they taste. They are most effective when served simply. A flavoured pasta – or a combination of two or three – is ideal in this recipe, although it is also delicious with plain pasta. Choose the herbs to complement the flavour of the pasta: basil for tomato; parsley and/or chives for mushroom; basil, parsley or chives for spinach; dill for beetroot; mixed herbs or perhaps something assertive like tarragon for plain pasta.

225g / 8oz pasta – perhaps a flavoured one, or two or three different colours	25g / 1oz butter salt and freshly ground black pepper
bunch of fresh herbs	fresh Parmesan cheese, grated (optional)

1 First fill a saucepan with 2 litres/3½ pints of water and bring to the boil. Add the pasta to the pan then let it bubble away, uncovered, for about 8 minutes or until it is *al dente*.

2 While the pasta is cooking, wash and chop the herbs – you need about 4 tablespoons.

3 Drain the pasta then put it back into the still-warm pan with the butter, herbs and some salt and pepper to taste. Mix gently, then serve out on to warmed plates, with fresh Parmesan if you wish.

SERVES 2

SUMMER SPAGHETTI WITH AVOCADO

This is good served with some hot garlic bread and a leafy summer salad.

450g / 1lb tomatoes	1 avocado
175g / 6oz spaghetti	lemon juice
2 tbls olive oil	6–8 large basil leaves
1 garlic clove, crushed	freshly grated
salt and freshly ground black pepper	Parmesan cheese (optional)

1 First fill a saucepan with 2 litres/3½ pints of water and bring to the boil for the pasta.

2 Put the tomatoes into a bowl, cover with boiling water and leave for a few seconds until the

skins split. Drain, cover with cold water and slip off the skins with a sharp knife. Chop the tomatoes roughly, removing any hard bits of core.

3 When the water boils, add the spaghetti and cook, uncovered, for about 8 minutes, until *al dente*.

4 Heat the oil in a large saucepan, add the garlic and cook over a moderate heat for 1–2 minutes. Add the chopped tomatoes and salt and pepper to taste and heat gently, just to warm through. Peel, stone and chop the avocado and toss it in a little lemon juice.

5 Drain the pasta and return it to the still-warm saucepan. Add the tomato mixture and the avocado and toss well to mix, then tear in the basil, check the seasoning, and serve. Hand round Parmesan cheese separately, if you like.

SERVES 2

PASTA WITH GARLIC AND HERB MAYONNAISE

You can make this less rich by replacing some of the mayonnaise with plain yogurt, if you like. Summery and easy to prepare, it can be served either hot or cold. A simple salad goes well with it, and/or some warm bread.

225g / 8oz pasta, such
  as conchiglie
bunch of fresh herbs
4 tbls mayonnaise, a
  good bought one such
  as Hellman's, or
  mayonnaise and
  plain yogurt mixed

1 garlic clove, crushed
salt and freshly
  ground black pepper
fresh Parmesan cheese,
  grated (optional)

1 First fill a saucepan with 2 litres/3½ pints of water and bring to the boil. Add the pasta to the pan, then cook, uncovered, for about 8 minutes or until it is *al dente*.

2 While the pasta is cooking, wash and chop the herbs – you need about 4 tablespoons.

3 Drain the pasta then put it back into the still-warm pan. Add the mayonnaise, or mayonnaise and yogurt, and the herbs and garlic. Mix gently, season with salt and pepper, then serve out on to warmed plates, with fresh Parmesan if you wish.

SERVES 2

FUSILLI WITH FENNEL AND MANGETOUT

225g / 8oz fennel bulb
125g / 4oz mangetout
  or sugar-snap peas
15g / ½oz butter
175g / 6oz fusilli

salt and freshly
  ground black pepper
fresh Parmesan cheese,
  grated (optional)

1 First fill a saucepan with 2 litres/3½ pints of water and bring to the boil for the pasta.

2 Next prepare the vegetables: trim off any tough outer leaves and stems from the fennel, reserving any green leafy bits for garnish. Wash and slice the fennel; wash, top and tail the mangetout or peas.

3 Cook the fennel in 5 cm/2 inches of boiling water for about 7 minutes, until it is almost tender, then put in the mangetout or sugar-snap peas and cook for a further 2 minutes. Drain, add the butter and leave on one side.

4 When the water boils, add the pasta to the pan, then let it bubble away, uncovered, for about 8 minutes or until it is *al dente*.

5 Just before the pasta is ready, gently reheat the vegetables, then drain the pasta and return it to the still-warm saucepan. Add the vegetables and snip in any reserved leafy bits of fennel. Check the seasoning and serve, with Parmesan cheese if you like.

SERVES 2

CAVATAPPI WITH SPINACH, RAISINS AND PINE NUTS

I love this mixture of contrasting flavours and textures; the sweetness of the raisins and the crunchiness of the toasted pine nuts complement the spinach and pasta perfectly. Cavatappi is a corkscrew-shaped pasta, but if you can't find it you can use fusilli instead.

450g / 1lb tender fresh spinach or frozen leaf spinach
25g / 1oz raisins
40g / 1½oz butter
175g / 6oz cavatappi or similar pasta
25g / 1oz pine nuts
salt and freshly ground black pepper
freshly grated nutmeg
fresh Parmesan cheese, grated

1 First fill a saucepan with 2 litres/3½ pints of water and bring to the boil for the pasta.

2 Next prepare the spinach: if you are using fresh spinach, wash it in two or three changes of water and remove any tough stems. Put the fresh or frozen spinach into a saucepan and cook over a high heat until the spinach has wilted and is tender. If the frozen spinach is very solid you may need to add a few tablespoons of water to the pan to prevent it sticking. Drain the spinach, add the raisins and half the butter and leave on one side until the pasta is done.

3 When the water boils, add the pasta to the pan, then let it bubble away, uncovered, for about 8 minutes or until it is *al dente*. While the pasta is cooking, toast the pine nuts under a hot grill; keep your eye on them as they only take 1–2 minutes and can quickly burn. When they are golden brown, remove them from the grill and keep on one side.

4 Just before the pasta is ready, gently reheat the spinach. Drain the pasta, return it to the still-warm saucepan with the rest of the butter and add the spinach mixture and the toasted pine nuts. Season with salt, pepper and freshly grated nutmeg and serve at once on to warmed plates. Hand round the Parmesan cheese separately.

SERVES 2

FUSILLI WITH COURGETTES AND TOMATOES

225g / 8oz courgettes
225g / 8oz tomatoes
175g / 6oz fusilli
2 tbls olive oil
1 garlic clove, crushed
salt and freshly ground black pepper
6 large basil leaves
fresh Parmesan cheese

1 First fill a saucepan with 2 litres/3½ pints of water and bring to the boil for the pasta.

2 Next prepare the vegetables: wash the courgettes and cut them into rounds or matchsticks. Put the tomatoes into a bowl, cover with boiling water and leave for a few seconds until the skins split. Drain, cover with cold water and slip off the skins with a sharp knife. Chop the tomatoes into chunky pieces, removing any tough pieces around the stem.

3 When the water boils, add the pasta to the pan, then let it bubble away, uncovered, for about 8 minutes or until it is *al dente*.

4 While the pasta is cooking, heat the oil in a large saucepan and add the courgettes and garlic. Cook over a moderate heat, stirring often, for about 4 minutes or until the courgettes are just tender, then add the tomatoes and salt and pepper to taste.

5 Just before the pasta is ready, gently reheat the courgette mixture then drain the pasta and return it to the still-warm saucepan. Stir the courgettes and tomatoes into the pasta; tear in the basil, check the seasoning, and top with some flaked or freshly grated Parmesan cheese.

SERVES 2

OPPOSITE: **(top)** *Spinach Tagliatelle with Walnuts, page 64, and (bottom) Fusilli with Courgettes and Tomatoes*

CHEESE & CREAM SAUCES
✳

SPINACH TAGLIATELLE WITH WALNUTS

This is a rich pasta dish which only needs a simple salad accompaniment: a fresh tomato and basil salad or a green salad, such as oak-leaf lettuce, with a very light dressing would be nice.

15g / ½ oz butter	salt and freshly
1 onion, peeled and	ground black pepper
chopped	225g / 8oz spinach
1 garlic clove, crushed	tagliatelle
150ml / 5fl oz double	25–50g / 1–2oz
cream	walnuts, chopped

To make a light balsamic vinegar vinaigrette to serve two people, mix 1 tablespoon of olive oil, 1 teaspoon of balsamic vinegar and some seasoning in a salad bowl. Put the salad leaves on top and toss just before you are ready to eat.

1 First fill a saucepan with 2 litres/3½ pints of water and bring to the boil for the pasta.

2 Next start making the sauce: melt the butter in a small saucepan then put in the onion, cover and cook gently for 10 minutes, until tender but not brown. Stir in the garlic, cook for 1–2 minutes, then stir in the cream.

3 Let the mixture simmer gently for about 10 minutes, until the cream has reduced a bit and thickened, then season well with salt and pepper. Keep on one side until the pasta is done.

4 When the water boils, add the pasta to the pan, then let it bubble away, uncovered, for about 8 minutes or until it is *al dente*.

5 Just before the pasta is ready, gently reheat the sauce. Drain the pasta, return it to the still-warm saucepan and season with some salt, then add the sauce and most of the walnuts and stir so that all the pasta gets coated. Serve out on to warm plates with the remaining nuts sprinkled on top.

SERVES 2

TAGLIATELLE AL DOLCELATTE

Very quick and easy, this can be made with other blue cheeses, such as Gorgonzola, if you prefer. You can use single or double cream, depending on how rich you want it to be. A simple green salad, perhaps with some thin rings of red onion and a light balsamic vinegar vinaigrette, goes well with this.

75g / 3oz Dolcelatte	salt and freshly
cheese	ground black pepper
150ml / 5fl oz single	225g / 8oz tagliatelle
cream	fresh Parmesan cheese,
15g / ½ oz butter	grated

1 First fill a saucepan with 2 litres/3½ pints of water and bring to the boil for the pasta.

2 Next start making the sauce: crumble the Dolcelatte into a saucepan and add the cream and butter. Heat gently, stirring, until the ingredients have melted together and formed a sauce. Remove from the heat and season with salt and pepper.

3 When the water boils, add the pasta to the pan, then let it bubble away, uncovered, for about 8 minutes or until it is *al dente*.

4 Just before the pasta is ready, gently reheat the sauce. Drain the pasta, return it to the still-warm saucepan and season with some salt; then add the sauce and stir so that all the pasta gets coated. Serve out on to warm plates and hand round the Parmesan separately.

SERVES 2

PAPPARDELLE WITH CREAM AND PARMESAN

This delicious and simple pasta dish is rich, but can be enjoyed as part of a healthy diet if you serve it as a main course with a simple salad of leaves or ripe plum tomatoes and keep the rest of the day's meals free from fat: balance is the key. I love this made with wide ribbon pasta – pappardelle – but you could use a lighter, finer ribbon type such as tagliatelle or fettuccine, if you prefer. Really good freshly grated Parmesan cheese makes all the difference to this recipe.

175–225g / 6–8oz pappardelle	salt and freshly ground black pepper
25g / 1oz butter	50g / 2oz fresh Parmesan cheese, grated
150ml / 5fl oz double cream	

1. Fill a saucepan with 2 litres/3½ pints of water and bring to the boil. Add the pasta and cook uncovered, for about 8 minutes, until it is *al dente*.
2. Just before the pasta is ready, put the butter and cream into a small saucepan and heat gently until the butter has melted into the cream.
3. Drain the pasta, return it to the still-warm saucepan and season with salt. Pour in the cream mixture and add the Parmesan cheese. Check the seasoning, adding plenty of freshly ground black pepper, then serve at once on to warmed plates.
SERVES 2

FARFALLE WITH NO-COOK MASCARPONE SAUCE

Another almost-instant pasta dish, which you can flavour in any way you please – try chopped fresh herbs, crushed garlic, sun-dried tomatoes, or simply lots of coarsely ground black pepper. It's quite rich, so a refreshing salad – tomato and basil is my favourite – is all the accompaniment it needs.

225g / 8oz farfalle	salt and freshly ground black pepper
125g / 4oz mascarpone cheese	fresh Parmesan cheese (optional)
freshly grated nutmeg	

1. Fill a saucepan with 2 litres/3½ pints of water and bring to the boil. Add the pasta then cook, uncovered, for about 8 minutes, until it is *al dente*.
2. Drain the pasta then put it back into the pan. Add the mascarpone and some nutmeg and mix gently. Season well, then serve topped with some flaked or freshly grated Parmesan if you wish.
SERVES 2

CONCHIGLIE WITH RICOTTA AND SPINACH

175g / 6oz conchiglie	salt and freshly ground black pepper
225g / 8oz tender fresh spinach or frozen leaf spinach	freshly grated nutmeg
1 tbls olive oil	fresh Parmesan cheese, grated
1 garlic clove, crushed	
125g / 4oz ricotta cheese	

1. First fill a saucepan with 2 litres/3½ pints of water and bring to the boil. Add the pasta and cook, uncovered, for about 8 minutes, or until *al dente*.
2. If you're using fresh spinach, wash it in two or three changes of water, removing any tough stems.
3. Heat the oil in a saucepan and put in the garlic. Cook for a few seconds, then add the spinach and cook over a high heat until the spinach has wilted and is tender. If the frozen spinach is very solid it will take a bit longer and you will need to watch it carefully to make sure it doesn't stick.
4. Drain the conchiglie, return it to the pan and gently stir in the spinach and the ricotta. Season with salt, pepper and freshly grated nutmeg and serve at once, with Parmesan cheese.
SERVES 2

Small pasta shapes work best for this recipe – farfalle, fusilli or lumache, for instance.

MACARONI CHEESE

Macaroni cheese is so popular with my daughter Claire and her friends that I get tired of making it, though they never seem to get tired of eating it. I try to vary it by adding different ingredients. In this version tomatoes add freshness and moisture as well as colour. I would serve it with watercress or, for the children, probably frozen peas (and tomato ketchup!).

75g / 3oz quick-cooking macaroni
1 or 2 medium to large tomatoes
breadcrumbs made from 1 small slice of stale bread
1 tbls finely grated Parmesan cheese

FOR THE CHEESE SAUCE
25g / 1oz butter
25g / 1oz plain flour
300ml / ½ pint semi-skimmed milk
½ tsp mustard powder
3 tbls finely grated Parmesan cheese
salt and freshly ground black pepper

1 Bring a large saucepan of water to the boil, add the macaroni then cook, uncovered, for about 8 minutes or until the macaroni is *al dente*.

2 Meanwhile, make the cheese sauce: melt the butter in a saucepan and stir in the flour. When it froths, stir in about a third of the milk then beat well, over the heat, until it thickens. Repeat until all the milk has been used. Don't worry if it goes lumpy; just keep beating and all will be well.

3 Let the sauce simmer gently for a few minutes. Blend the mustard powder with a little water and add to the sauce, with the cheese and seasoning.

4 Heat the grill. When the macaroni is done, drain and add to the sauce. Check the seasoning, adding more salt and pepper if necessary.

5 Slice the tomatoes. Put the macaroni cheese into a shallow heatproof dish then cover with the tomato slices. Top with a light scattering of breadcrumbs and the cheese. Grill for a few minutes until the topping is golden brown.

SERVES 2

OPPOSITE: *(top) Fettuccine with Asparagus Sauce and (bottom) Macaroni Cheese*

FETTUCCINE WITH ASPARAGUS SAUCE

This is a lovely summery pasta dish; a salad of lettuce and fresh herbs goes well with it.

15g / ½ oz butter
1 onion, peeled and chopped
1 garlic clove, crushed
150ml / 5fl oz double cream

salt and freshly ground black pepper
freshly grated nutmeg
125–225g / 4–8oz asparagus spears
225g / 8oz fettuccine

1 First fill a saucepan with 2 litres/3½ pints of water and bring to the boil for the pasta.

2 Next start making the sauce: melt the butter in a small saucepan then put in the onion, cover and cook gently for 10 minutes, until tender but not brown. Stir in the garlic, cook for 1–2 minutes, then stir in the cream. Let the mixture simmer gently for about 10 minutes, until the cream has reduced a bit and thickened. Season with salt, pepper and freshly grated nutmeg and keep on one side until the pasta is done.

3 While the sauce is cooking, trim the asparagus, removing the ends of the stems if they are tough and cutting it into 2.5 cm/1 inch lengths. Keep the tips separate from the stems.

4 Bring 2.5 cm/1 inch of water to the boil in a pan and put in the chopped asparagus stems. Boil for 2 minutes, then add the tips, cover and cook for a further 2 minutes, or until they are beginning to get tender but are still crunchy. Drain well, then stir into the cream sauce, reserving a few of the asparagus tips.

5 When the water boils, add the pasta to the pan, and let it bubble away, uncovered, for about 8 minutes or until it is *al dente*.

6 Just before the pasta is ready, gently reheat the sauce. Drain the pasta, return it to the still-warm saucepan and season with some salt; then add the sauce and stir so that all the pasta gets coated.

7 Serve out on to warm plates with the reserved asparagus tips on top, and grind on some additional coarse black pepper if liked.

SERVES 2

TAGLIATELLE WITH INSTANT GARLIC AND CHEESE SAUCE

225g / 8oz tagliatelle
1 × 125g / 4oz packet
  of garlic and herb
  cream cheese

salt and freshly
  ground black pepper

1 Fill a saucepan with 2 litres/3½ pints of water and bring to the boil then add the pasta and cook, uncovered, for about 8 minutes, until it is *al dente*.
2 Drain the pasta then put it back in the pan. Gently mix in the garlic and herb cream cheese, season well, then serve out on to warmed plates.
SERVES 2

FUSILLI WITH LEMON, CREAM AND PEAS

I think of this as a summer recipe, but it's also lovely in the winter, bringing a feeling of sunshine with it.

15g / ½oz butter
1 onion, peeled and
  chopped
1 garlic clove, crushed
150ml / 5fl oz double
  or single cream
grated rind of ½ lemon

salt and freshly
  ground black pepper
175g / 6oz fusilli
125g / 4oz fresh
  podded peas, or fresh
  or frozen petits pois
6 basil leaves

1 First fill a saucepan with 2 litres/3½ pints of water and bring to the boil for the pasta.
2 Meanwhile, melt the butter in a pan then put in the onion, cover and cook for 10 minutes, until tender but not brown. Stir in the garlic and cook for 1–2 minutes longer, then stir in the cream and simmer gently for 10 minutes, until it has reduced a bit and thickened. Add the lemon rind and seasoning.
3 When the water boils, add the pasta to the pan, and cook, uncovered, for 8 minutes, until *al dente*.

4 Cook the peas in a little boiling water for 2–3 minutes or until they are just tender, then drain.
5 Just before the pasta is ready, gently reheat the sauce and add the peas. Drain the pasta, return it to the pan and add some salt, then stir in the sauce. Tear in the basil leaves, stir again, then serve.
SERVES 2

CONCHIGLIE WITH COURGETTES AND CREAM

15g / ½oz butter
1 onion, peeled and
  chopped
1 garlic clove, crushed
150 ml / 5fl oz double
  or single cream
salt and freshly
  ground black pepper

175g / 6oz conchiglie
225g / 8oz courgettes
small bunch of chervil
  or parsley
lemon juice

1 First fill a saucepan with 2 litres/3½ pints of water and bring to the boil for the pasta.
2 Meanwhile, melt the butter in a pan then put in the onion, cover and cook gently for 10 minutes, until tender but not brown. Add the garlic and cook for 1–2 minutes longer, then stir in the cream and simmer gently for about 10 minutes, until it has reduced a bit and thickened. Season to taste.
3 When the water boils, add the pasta to the pan and cook, uncovered, for 8 minutes, until *al dente*.
4 Slice the courgettes, then cook them in a little boiling water for about 2 minutes, until just tender but still slightly crisp. Drain and add to the sauce.
5 Wash and chop the chervil or parsley – you need about 2 tablespoons.
6 Just before the pasta is ready, gently reheat the sauce. Drain the pasta, return it to the pan and add some salt; then stir in the sauce and the herbs. Add a little lemon juice to sharpen the sauce then serve out on to warmed plates.
SERVES 2

FARFALLE WITH CREAMY BROCCOLI SAUCE

The cream sauce in this case is a Béchamel. For a lighter version, leave out the cream and use semi-skimmed milk.

25g / 1oz butter
20g / ¾ oz plain flour
300ml / ½ pint milk
1 bay leaf
a few stalks of
    parsley, if available
slice of onion, if
    available

175g / 6oz farfalle
225g / 8oz broccoli
salt and freshly
    ground black pepper
4 tbls cream (optional)
freshly grated nutmeg

1 First fill a saucepan with 2 litres/3½ pints of water and bring to the boil for the pasta.

2 Meanwhile, make the sauce: melt the butter in a saucepan and stir in the flour. When it froths, stir in half the milk and beat well, over the heat, until it thickens, then stir in the rest of the milk and keep stirring vigorously over the heat until the sauce is thick and smooth. Add the bay leaf, along with the parsley stalks and slice of onion if you have them, then contine to cook the sauce over a very low heat.

3 When the water boils, add the pasta then let it bubble away, uncovered, for about 8 minutes, until it is *al dente*.

4 Wash the broccoli then break or chop the florets into bite-sized pieces and peel and slice into matchsticks any of the stem that is tender enough to use. Cook the broccoli in 5 cm/2 inches of boiling water for 3–4 minutes, until it is just tender. Drain and keep it warm.

5 Drain the pasta and return it to the saucepan. Add the broccoli and season with some salt. Remove the bay leaf, onion and parsley from the sauce, scraping as much sauce off them as you can, then discard them. If you're using the cream, stir this into the sauce over the heat, and season with salt, pepper and freshly grated nutmeg to taste.

6 Pour the sauce in with the pasta and broccoli, stir gently to mix, then serve.
SERVES 2

FETTUCCINE WITH CREAM AND HERB SAUCE

This sauce can be made with either single or double cream, depending on how rich you want it to be. (It's most delicious with double cream, I have to say, but it does work with single cream.) You can use almost any fresh herbs: I like chervil, parsley and chives, or tarragon for a more assertive flavour.

15g / ½ oz butter
1 onion, peeled and
    chopped
1 garlic clove, crushed
150ml / 5fl oz double
    or single cream

salt and freshly
    ground black pepper
freshly grated nutmeg
bunch of mixed fresh
    herbs
225g / 8oz fettuccine

1 First fill a saucepan with 2 litres/3½ pints of water and bring to the boil for the pasta.

2 Next start making the sauce: melt the butter in a small saucepan then put in the onion, cover and cook gently for 10 minutes, until tender but not brown. Add the garlic and cook for 1–2 minutes longer, then stir in the cream and leave the mixture to simmer gently for about 10 minutes, until the cream has reduced a bit and thickened. Season with salt, pepper and freshly grated nutmeg and keep on one side until the pasta is done.

3 While the sauce is cooking, wash and chop the herbs – you need about 2–4 tablespoons.

4 When the water boils, add the fettuccine to the pan and let it bubble away, uncovered, for about 8 minutes or until it is *al dente*.

5 Just before the pasta is ready, gently reheat the sauce. Drain the fettuccine, return it to the still-warm saucepan and season with some salt; then add the sauce and most of the herbs and stir so that all the pasta gets coated. Serve out on to warm plates with the remaining herbs scattered on top.
SERVES 2

Freshly grated nutmeg is a useful flavouring: buy a nutmeg grater and some whole nutmegs – they can be grated in moments.

PULSES,GRAINS & NUTS

These are packed full of nutrients. Nuts are a very concentrated source of energy, and small quantities go a long way. They make a wonderful fast food – great for putting into lunchboxes with some salad or fruit for a nourishing, fastest-ever meal. Most pulses need soaking and long cooking, so all the recipes in this book rely on canned ones to save time, except for split red lentils which cook quickly without soaking. Grains are invaluable, too, and are much richer in protein, minerals and vitamins than many people realize.

BEANS & LENTILS
✳

CHICK PEA BROTH WITH PARSLEY DUMPLINGS

This is cheap, comforting, tasty and quick to make: what more can one ask of a simple recipe? The dumplings are based on one of Nigel Slater's recipes.

2 onions
4 garlic cloves
4 carrots
4 celery stalks
2 tbls oil
2 × 425g / 15oz cans
  chick peas
salt and freshly
  ground black pepper

FOR THE DUMPLINGS
200g / 7oz plain flour
2 tsp baking powder
1 tsp salt
50g / 2oz Cheddar
  cheese, grated
4–6 tbls chopped fresh
  parsley
1 egg
about 100ml / 4fl oz
  milk

1   Peel and chop the onions; peel and crush the garlic; scrape the carrots and cut them into thin rounds; trim and dice the celery. The vegetables need to be cut up small so that they will cook quickly.

2   Heat the oil in a large saucepan and cook the vegetables, with a lid on the pan, for 5 minutes. Then add the chick peas, together with their liquid, 1.7 litres/3 pints of water and some salt and pepper. Cover and leave to simmer for 15–20 minutes.

3   Meanwhile, make the dumplings: sift the flour and baking powder into a bowl and add the salt, grated cheese and parsley. Whisk the egg and stir that in, along with enough milk to make a soft but not sticky dough. Form the dough into eight balls and drop these into the soup.

4   Cover the pan and leave to cook for 10–12 minutes, until the dumplings are puffed up, light and cooked through, and all the vegetables are tender.
SERVES 4

TUSCAN BEAN SOUP

This soup makes a good light meal on its own with some bread, or serve it with some crostini (see pages 12–14) and a chunky little gem lettuce salad for a more substantial meal.

1 tbls olive oil
1 onion, peeled and
  chopped
2 garlic cloves,
  crushed
1 × 425g / 15oz can
  cannellini beans

salt and freshly
  ground black pepper
lemon juice
extra virgin olive oil
  (optional)
roughly chopped flat-
  leaf parsley

1   Heat the oil in a large saucepan, add the onion then cover and cook gently for 10 minutes, until tender but not brown. Stir in the garlic and cook for 1–2 minutes longer.

2   Add the cannellini beans, together with their liquid, then purée in a food processor or blender until fairly smooth and creamy.

3   Return the mixture to the pan and add some water to adjust the consistency to your liking: about 300ml/½ pint makes a medium-thick soup. Bring to the boil then season with salt and pepper and a squeeze or two of lemon juice.

4   Serve the soup in warmed bowls, topped with some extra virgin olive oil, if you like, some flat-leaf parsley and coarsely ground black pepper.
SERVES 2

A few drops of lemon juice, added at the end of cooking, perk up many dishes in a magical way. But it must be freshly squeezed – other types don't have the same effect. Any leftover juice can be frozen in an ice-cube container.

SPICY LENTIL SOUP

1 tbls oil	pinch of chilli powder
1 onion, peeled and	1 bay leaf
chopped	175g / 6oz split red
8–10 cardamom pods	lentils
2 garlic cloves,	juice of ½–1 lemon
crushed	salt and freshly
1½ tsp turmeric	ground black pepper

1 Heat the oil in a large saucepan, then add the onion, cover and cook gently for 5–7 minutes.

2 Meanwhile, bruise the cardamom pods in a pestle and mortar or with a wooden spoon. Add them to the onion, along with the garlic, turmeric, chilli powder and bay leaf, and cook over a gentle heat for a further 2–3 minutes.

3 Stir in the lentils, then pour in 750ml/ 1½ pints of water. Bring to the boil and simmer, uncovered, for 20–25 minutes, until the lentils are very tender and pale coloured.

4 Sharpen the flavour with lemon juice to taste, season with salt and pepper, then serve accompanied by poppadums if you like.

SERVES 2

BUTTERBEAN AND TOMATO SOUP

Butterbean and tomato is a combination I remember from my vegetarian childhood and I still think it's good. Cheesy garlic bread or bruschetta (see pages 12–14) go well with it.

1 tbls olive oil or oil	1 × 425g / 15oz can
from a jar of	butterbeans
sun-dried tomatoes	3–4 sun-dried
1 onion, peeled and	tomatoes
chopped	salt and freshly
1 garlic clove, crushed	ground black pepper
1 × 400g / 14oz can	
tomatoes	

1 Heat the oil in a large saucepan then add the onion, cover and cook gently for 5 minutes, until softened. Stir in the garlic and cook for 2 minutes, then pour in the canned tomatoes and the butterbeans, together with their liquid.

2 Chop the sun-dried tomatoes and add these to the pan. Simmer, uncovered, for about 10 minutes.

3 You can serve the soup as it is, but I think it's nicest if you purée half of it in a food processor or blender then stir it back in, because this gives a slightly thickened, creamy consistency. Season with salt and pepper and serve.

SERVES 2

PROVENCAL FLAGEOLET BEAN SOUP

This is light yet filling, and the pesto gives it a sunny Mediterranean flavour. It's good with some warm granary bread or hot garlic bread.

125g / 4oz carrot	1 garlic clove, crushed
1 tbls olive oil	1 × 425g / 15oz can
1 onion, peeled and	flageolet beans
chopped	1–2 tbls pesto
125g / 4oz leek	salt and freshly
125g / 4oz courgettes	ground black pepper

1 Scrape the carrot then cut it into tiny dice (about 6 mm/¼ inch) so that it will cook quickly. Heat the oil in a large saucepan and fry the onion and carrot, with a lid on the pan, for 5 minutes, until beginning to soften. Wash, trim and finely slice the leek; wash, trim and dice the courgettes.

2 Add the leek and the garlic to the pan; cover and cook for a further 5 minutes, then add the courgettes, flageolet beans and 600ml/1 pint of water. Bring to the boil and simmer for about 10 minutes until the vegetables are tender.

3 Stir in pesto to taste and season with salt and pepper, then serve.

SERVES 2

LENTIL CHILLI BURGERS WITH DILL SAUCE

This is a pleasant combination of hot and cool, crisp and creamy. Serve with a simple salad or a steamed vegetable such as broccoli. The burgers are nicest if they are deep-fried, which you can do quickly in a medium saucepan rather than going through all the rigmarole of getting out a deep-fryer – or they can be shallow-fried.

1 onion, peeled and
  chopped
1 tbls olive oil
1 garlic clove, crushed
1 fresh green chilli,
  de-seeded and
  chopped, or chilli
  powder to taste
2 tsp ground coriander
1 × 425g / 15oz can
  green lentils, drained
oil for deep- or
  shallow-frying
1 slice white or whole-
  wheat bread, crusts
  removed

1 packet fresh
  coriander, chopped
salt and freshly
  ground black pepper
1 egg, beaten
4 tbls dried
  breadcrumbs

FOR THE SAUCE
2–3 tbls chopped fresh
  dill
150ml / 5fl oz creamy
  yogurt

1. Fry the onion in the oil, with a lid on the pan, for 5 minutes. Add the garlic, chilli and ground coriander then cover and cook for 2–3 minutes. Remove from the heat and stir in the lentils.
2. If you are going to deep-fry the burgers, put the oil on to heat, but keep your eye on it. Cover the bread with water, drain immediately, then squeeze out all the water and crumble the bread – this is a quick way of making breadcrumbs. Add to the lentil mixture along with the fresh coriander and seasoning, mashing the mixture with the spoon or a potato masher so that it holds together.
3. Divide the mixture into four and form into sphere shapes if you are going to deep-fry them, or flattish burger shapes for shallow-frying.
4. Dip the burgers first in the beaten egg, then in the dried breadcrumbs, making sure they are well coated. Then fry them until crisp and brown: they will need about 3–4 minutes on each side if shallow-frying and 4–5 minutes in total if deep-frying. Drain them well on kitchen paper.
5. Serve with a sauce made by stirring the chopped dill into the creamy yogurt and seasoning with salt and pepper.
SERVES 2

LENTILS WITH GRILLED PEPPERS

This is a very pleasant combination of flavours, textures and colours: so simple, but so good. I like a green salad with it and some good light bread, such as ciabatta.

1 large red pepper
1 large yellow pepper
1 × 425g / 15oz can
  green or brown
  lentils

2 tbls balsamic
  vinegar
salt and freshly
  ground black pepper
sprigs of basil

1. Cut the peppers into quarters, place them cut-side down on a grill pan and grill them on high for 10 minutes or until the skins have blistered and charred in places. Remove from the grill and cover with a damp cloth.
2. Meanwhile, gently heat the lentils, in their liquid, in a saucepan.
3. When the peppers are cool enough to handle, pull off the skin with a sharp knife, discard the seeds and stalks, cut the flesh into strips and put into a serving dish.
4. Drain the lentils and add to the peppers with the balsamic vinegar, salt and pepper to taste, and some torn basil leaves.
SERVES 2

OPPOSITE: *(left) Lentil Chilli Burgers with Dill Sauce, (above) Provençal Flageolet Bean Soup, page 73, (right) Lentils with Grilled Peppers*

LENTILS WITH CORIANDER AND HARD-BOILED EGGS

Hard-boiled eggs and lentils are one of those classic combinations, like tomato and basil or bread and cheese – and a colourful and nutritious pair they are too. Serve this on its own or with some rice, bread or chutney – it's very versatile, so please yourself!

If you can get the little Puy lentils, which cook in 40 minutes, you can use them for this recipe instead of canned green lentils. 100g / 3½ oz dried lentils is equivalent to a 425g / 15oz can. Cook the lentils in plenty of boiling water until tender.

2 eggs
1 tbls olive oil
1 onion, peeled and
  sliced
1 garlic clove, crushed
2 tsp ground coriander

1 × 425g / 15oz can
  green lentils, drained
2 tbls chopped fresh
  coriander
salt and freshly
  ground black pepper

1 Hard-boil the eggs by simmering them in a pan of boiling water for 7–10 minutes. Then drain them, cover with cold water and leave to cool.
2 Heat the olive oil in a pan, add the onion and garlic then cover and cook gently for 5 minutes, until softened.
3 Add the ground coriander to the onion and garlic, stirring for 1–2 minutes, then put in the lentils and leave to cook very gently until the lentils are thoroughly heated. Meanwhile, shell the hard-boiled eggs, rinse them under cold water, then slice them.
4 Add the chopped fresh coriander to the lentil mixture, taste and season with salt and pepper. Serve the lentils and the eggs together: you could stir the eggs into the lentil mixture if you wish, or just arrange them around it attractively.
SERVES 2

CHICK PEA CROQUETTES WITH CORIANDER RAITA

These are crisp on the outside, moist and spicy within, lovely with a yogurt raita and a fresh salad – perhaps diced cucumber and chopped spring onion. You really do need a food processor to purée the chick peas for this recipe.

1 onion, peeled and
  chopped
1 tbls olive oil
1 garlic clove, crushed
1 tsp cumin seeds
1 × 425g / 15oz can
  chick peas, drained
salt and freshly
  ground black pepper
1 egg, beaten

4 tbls dried
  breadcrumbs
oil for shallow-frying

FOR THE RAITA
2 tbls chopped fresh
  coriander
150ml / 5fl oz creamy
  yogurt

1 Fry the onion in the oil, with a lid on the pan, for 5 minutes, until beginning to soften, then add the garlic and cumin seeds and fry for a further 2–3 minutes. Remove from the heat.
2 Put the onion mixture into a food processor. Drain the chick peas, reserving the liquid, then add them to the food processor and whizz to form a thick purée that holds together. If necessary, add a little of the reserved chick pea liquid to obtain the right consistency, but be careful not to let the mixture get too moist.
3 Season with salt and pepper, then divide the mixture into four and form into flattish croquettes; don't make them too thick or the inside won't heat through properly.
4 Dip the croquettes first in the beaten egg then in the dried breadcrumbs, making sure they are well coated. Then heat the oil in a frying pan and shallow-fry the croquettes for 3–4 minutes on each side, until crisp and brown. Drain them well on kitchen paper.
5 Serve with a raita made by stirring the chopped coriander into the creamy yogurt and seasoning with salt and pepper.
SERVES 2

CHICK PEA PUREE WITH SPICED ONION TOPPING

This is so simple to make, and good with some warm bread and perhaps a cucumber and tomato salad with some chopped fresh coriander and slices of lemon.

2 onions, peeled and
  chopped
2 tbls olive oil
2 garlic cloves,
  crushed
2 tsp ground coriander

1 tsp ground cumin
1 × 425g / 15oz can
  chick peas
salt and freshly
  ground black pepper

1 Fry the onions in the oil, with a lid on the pan, for 5 minutes or until beginning to soften, then add the garlic, coriander and cumin.

2 Cover and fry for a further 2–3 minutes, then take out a third of the mixture and put it into a food processor. Continue to cook the rest of the onions and spices until the onions are brown, but don't have the heat too high or the spices might burn.

3 Meanwhile, put the chick peas and about half of their liquid into the food processor with the onions. Whizz to a purée, adding more of the liquid if necessary to make a thick but creamy mixture.

4 Season with salt and pepper, then transfer the purée to a pan and heat through. Serve topped with the crisp, browned spicy onion mixture.

SERVES 2

RED BEAN BURGERS WITH SOURED CREAM SAUCE

Soured cream has the same fat content as single cream, so it's not over-rich when used in small quantities. However, for a lower-fat sauce plain yogurt is very good instead. Another option is to serve the burgers with a good dollop of guacamole (see page 21) or, of course, you could forget about a sauce altogether and serve the burgers in light rolls or with salad.

1 onion, peeled and
  chopped
1 tbls olive oil
1 garlic clove, crushed
1 tomato
75g / 3oz bread, crusts
  removed
1 × 425g / 15oz can red
  kidney beans,
  drained
salt and freshly
  ground black pepper

1 egg, beaten
4 tbls dried
  breadcrumbs
oil for shallow-frying

FOR THE SAUCE
2 tbls chopped fresh
  chives
150ml / 5fl oz soured
  cream

1 Fry the onion in the oil, with a lid on the pan, for 5 minutes, until beginning to soften. Add the garlic and fry for a further 2–3 minutes.

2 Meanwhile, pour boiling water over the tomato and leave for a few seconds until the skin splits, then slip off the skin with a sharp knife. De-seed and chop the tomato, removing any hard bits of core, then add it to the onion and garlic. Stir, then cook, uncovered for 3–4 minutes, until the tomato has cooked down a bit.

3 Remove the pan from the heat. Roughly tear the bread and add to the pan, together with the beans. The mixture has to be mashed very well at this stage to blend together all the ingredients, and the easiest way to do this is to tip it into a food processor and whizz it to a thick purée. You can do it by hand, however, with patience, elbow grease and a good strong potato masher.

4 Season the mixture with salt and pepper, then divide it into four and form into flattish burger shapes; don't make them too thick or the inside won't heat through.

5 Dip the burgers first in the beaten egg then in the dried breadcrumbs, making sure they are well coated. Then heat the oil in a frying pan and shallow-fry them for 3–4 minutes on each side, until they are crisp and brown. Drain them well on kitchen paper.

6 Serve the burgers straight away with a sauce made by stirring the chopped fresh chives into the soured cream and seasoning with salt and pepper to taste.

SERVES 2

Cumin (both whole and ground) and coriander (ground is most useful) are wonderful for flavouring pulses and vegetables.

ULTIMATE RED BEAN CHILLI

This quick chilli is good with bread, mashed potatoes, plain pasta or rice, or some potato wedges, soured cream and chives (see page 106). If there is any left over, it's nice cold as a salad, or stuffed into pitta bread, or as a filling for crêpes or tortillas.

1 tbls olive oil	1 large green chilli
1 onion, peeled and chopped	1 × 425g / 15oz can red kidney beans, drained
1 red pepper	salt and freshly ground black pepper
125g / 4oz carrot	chilli powder (optional)
1 garlic clove, crushed	
1 × 400g / 14oz can tomatoes	

1. Heat the oil in a medium-large saucepan, then put in the onion, cover and cook for 5 minutes.
2. De-seed and chop the red pepper; scrape and dice the carrot. Add to the pan with the garlic. Stir, then cover and cook for 10 minutes.
3. Stir the tomatoes into the mixture, breaking them up with the spoon. De-seed the chilli, slice it into rings and add it to the saucepan. Cook gently, uncovered, for 10–15 minutes or until the carrot is tender.
4. Put in the red kidney beans and cook for a further 1–2 minutes to heat them through. Season with salt and pepper and add a pinch or so of chilli powder if it needs more of a kick, then serve.
SERVES 2

RED BEANS WITH THYME AND COCONUT CREAM

This is a quick version of a West Indian recipe. It's very warming and good with some rice. I think brown rice goes best with it, but if you're doing that you'll need to get it started first to give it time to cook.

1 × 425g / 15oz can red kidney beans	1 tsp dried thyme or 1 tbls fresh thyme
1 onion, peeled and chopped	25g / 1oz creamed coconut
1 carrot, finely sliced	salt and freshly ground black pepper
1 garlic clove, crushed	

1. Tip the red kidney beans and their liquid into a pan, add 300ml/½ pint of water and heat gently.
2. Add the onion, carrot, garlic and thyme and let the mixture simmer gently for about 15 minutes, until the vegetables are tender.
3. Flake the creamed coconut or chop it finely and add it to the pan, stirring gently until it has melted. Then season with salt and pepper and serve.
SERVES 2

TWO-BEAN SALAD WITH GARLIC BREAD

2 × 425g / 15oz cans beans, choose 2 contrasting types	salt and freshly ground black pepper
1–2 tsp balsamic vinegar	2–4 tbls chopped fresh herbs, such as chives, parsley and chervil or tarragon
3 tbls olive oil or plain low-fat yogurt, or a mixture	few thin slices of red onion (optional)
½ tsp Dijon mustard (optional)	garlic bread (see page 28)

1. Drain the beans. Mix 1 teaspoon of balsamic vinegar with the oil and/or yogurt in a salad bowl. Taste, and add more vinegar if necessary. Add the mustard, if you're using this, and plenty of seasoning.
2. Add the beans, herbs and onion, if you're using this; stir gently then leave on one side while you prepare the garlic bread. Stir again before serving.
SERVES 4

OPPOSITE: *Ultimate Red Bean Chilli*

This is a very easy salad which can be varied as much as you like by using different dressings, different types of beans and additional ingredients. Hot garlic bread goes well with it. Any leftover salad will keep well for 24 hours, covered, in the fridge.

MEXICAN BEAN SALAD

1 small lettuce
4 tomatoes
1 small red pepper
1 tbls olive oil
1 onion, peeled and
 chopped
1 green chilli
1 garlic clove, crushed
1 × 425g / 15oz can red
 kidney beans,
 drained

salt and freshly
 ground black pepper
1 avocado
2 tbls chopped fresh
 chives
150ml / 5fl oz plain
 low-fat yogurt or
 soured cream
a few fresh coriander
 leaves, if available

1   Wash the lettuce and put it into a colander to drain. Put the tomatoes in a bowl, pour boiling water over them and leave for a few seconds until the skins split. Drain, cover with cold water and slip off the skins. Cut two of the tomatoes into eighths and chop the other two. Wash and slice the pepper, discarding the stem and seeds.

2   Heat the oil in a saucepan then add the onion, cover and cook over a moderate heat for 5 minutes, stirring occasionally.

3   Meanwhile, de-seed and chop the chilli, washing your hands carefully after handling it. Add the chilli, garlic and chopped tomatoes to the onion and cook for 5 minutes.

4   Add the beans to the onion mixture, mashing them roughly with a wooden spoon or a potato masher to give a chunky texture. Heat through, then season with salt and pepper and keep warm over a low heat.

5   Cover a large platter with the lettuce leaves and arrange the red pepper and tomato randomly on top.

6   Peel, stone and roughly chop the avocado. Stir the chives into the yogurt or soured cream.

7   Spoon the red bean mixture on to the centre of the salad. Sprinkle the chopped avocado over it, then drizzle some of the yogurt or soured cream mixture over everything – put the rest into a small bowl to serve with the salad. Serve the salad at once, garnished with fresh coriander leaves, if you have any.

SERVES 2

VARIATION

REFRIED BEANS WITH TORTILLA CHIPS

Omit the red pepper, 2 of the tomatoes and the avocado. Make the bean mixture as described above and stir some fresh coriander into it, if available. Transfer to a shallow heatproof dish and top with 150g/5oz tortilla chips and 125g/4oz Cheddar cheese, grated. Place under a hot grill to melt the cheese, then serve with the lettuce leaves (crisp ones are best) and the yogurt or soured cream mixture.

WHITE BEANS COOKED IN CREAM

This is rich and delicious, lovely for a treat, with fingers of toast and a green salad.

15g / ½oz butter
1 onion, peeled and
 chopped
1 garlic clove, crushed
150ml / 5fl oz single
 cream
1 × 425g / 15oz can
 white beans, such as
 haricot or cannellini

squeeze of lemon juice
salt and freshly
 ground black pepper
freshly grated nutmeg
fresh parsley

1   Melt the butter in a medium saucepan then put in the onion, cover and cook gently for 5 minutes, until tender but not brown.

2   Stir in the garlic and cook for 1–2 minutes longer, then stir in the cream and leave the mixture to simmer gently for about 5 minutes, until the cream has reduced a bit and thickened.

3   Drain the beans and add them to the pan. Heat gently, stirring often. Add the lemon juice and then season with salt, pepper and freshly grated nutmeg. Make sure the beans are really hot, then serve them out on to heated plates and snip a little parsley over the top.

SERVES 2

QUICK BEANY BAKE

There's nothing in the slightest bit gourmet about this recipe but it's adored by all kids. I think it originally came from a children's TV programme – my daughter Kate told it to me.

1 tbls olive oil
1 onion, peeled and
  chopped
225g / 8oz can baked
  beans
225g / 8oz can red
  kidney beans,
  drained

225g / 8oz can
  sweetcorn, drained
4–6 slices of bread
125g / 4oz cheese,
  grated

1. Heat the oil in a medium saucepan, then add the onion and cook, covered, for about 10 minutes, until it has softened.
2. Add the baked beans, kidney beans and sweetcorn to the pan. Cook the mixture gently until everything is hot.
3. Heat the grill. Transfer the beany mixture to a shallow heatproof dish that will fit under your grill. Roughly tear the slices of bread over the top (with or without the crusts) then cover with the grated cheese.
4. Grill for about 10 minutes, or until the bread is crisp and the cheese melted and golden brown. Serve at once.
SERVES 2–4

EASY VEGETABLE DAL

Soothing and colourful, this is enough for two to four people depending on what you serve with it – Indian breads and/or boiled rice make good accompaniments. Any that's left over tastes good, if not better, the next day. This recipe contains no fat and is a special favourite of mine for that reason, as well as for its flavour and comforting qualities.

200g / 7oz split red
  lentils
2 thin slices of fresh
  ginger root
½ tsp turmeric
1 tsp cumin seeds
1 tsp ground coriander
pinch of chilli powder

1 onion
2 carrots
1 garlic clove
125g / 4oz frozen peas
juice of ½ lemon
salt and freshly
  ground black pepper

1. Put the lentils, ginger root, turmeric, cumin seeds, ground coriander and chilli powder into a medium saucepan with 1 litre/1¾ pints of water and bring to the boil.
2. Meanwhile, peel and slice the onion, scrape or peel the carrots and slice them quite finely, and peel and crush the garlic. Add all these vegetables to the lentils as they continue to simmer away. Let the lentil mixture cook for about 25 minutes altogether. At first it will look hopelessly watery, then when it is done it will become thick and soft, like porridge, and all the vegetables should be tender, too.
3. Add the peas to the mixture and cook for a further 2–3 minutes, until they are heated through. Then stir in the lemon juice and season to taste with salt and pepper.
SERVES 2–4

SPLIT PEA AND OKRA DAL

This quick dal uses canned split peas and is good served with poppadums and some basmati rice. I sometimes add sliced tomatoes and a coriander raita (see page 76) for an easy Indian meal – much quicker than phoning the takeaway, as well as cheaper and less fatty.

1–2 tbls olive oil	½ tsp turmeric
2 onions, peeled and chopped	2 × 425g / 15oz cans yellow split peas
175g / 6oz okra	squeeze of lemon juice
1 green chilli	salt and freshly ground black pepper
1 garlic clove, crushed	
2 tsp cumin seeds	chopped fresh coriander (optional)
2 tsp ground coriander	

1 Heat the oil in a medium-large saucepan and put in the onions. Cook gently, with a lid on the pan, for 5 minutes.

2 Meanwhile, top and tail the okra and de-seed and chop the chilli. Add these to the pan, along with the garlic, cook for 2–3 minutes, then put in the cumin seeds, ground coriander and turmeric and stir over the heat for a minute or two.

3 Add the split peas to the vegetables, together with their liquid, then cook gently, uncovered, for 5–10 minutes or until the okra are tender and any wateriness has disappeared from the mixture.

4 Add the lemon juice and salt and pepper to taste and serve sprinkled with chopped fresh coriander, if you have it.

SERVES 4

OPPOSITE: *(left) Spiced Red Lentils and Potatoes with Caramelized Onions and (right) Split Pea and Okra Dal*

SPICED RED LENTILS AND POTATOES WITH CARAMELIZED ONIONS

This delicious spicy mixture evolved from the rather unpromising starting point of some potatoes and dried red lentils. It's good served with fresh chutney and a side salad.

125g / 4oz split red lentils	½ tsp grated fresh ginger root
225g / 8oz potatoes	15g / ½oz creamed coconut, flaked or chopped
2 onions, peeled and chopped	
1–2 tbls oil	squeeze of lemon juice
1 garlic clove, crushed	½ packet fresh coriander, chopped
½ tsp turmeric	salt and freshly ground black pepper
½ tsp black mustard seeds	paprika pepper

1 Put the lentils into a medium saucepan with 450ml/¾ pint of water. Bring to the boil, then leave to simmer, uncovered, for about 20 minutes.

2 Meanwhile, peel the potatoes and cut them into 2.5 cm/1 inch dice. Add these to the lentils after they have been cooking for 10 minutes. When the lentils are done – soft and pale-coloured – the potatoes should be just tender. Remove from the heat.

3 Fry the onions in 1 tablespoon of oil, with a lid on the pan, for 5 minutes, then remove half the onion and put on one side for the moment. Stir the garlic, turmeric, mustard seeds and ginger into the remaining onion in the pan, cover and cook for a further 4–5 minutes.

4 Add the onion and spice mixture and the creamed coconut to the lentils and stir gently until everything is combined and the coconut has melted. Then add the lemon juice, fresh coriander and a good seasoning of salt and pepper, and keep warm.

5 Put the remaining onion back in the pan, with more oil if necessary, and fry it over a moderate to high heat for 3–5 minutes, until golden brown and crisp. Serve the lentil mixture topped with the crisp onion and a sprinkling of paprika pepper.

SERVES 2

To make fresh chutney to serve with this, mix together some chopped tomato, chopped red onion and plenty of chopped fresh mint; add a squeeze of lemon juice, a dash of balsamic vinegar and seasoning to taste.

RICE
— ✳ —

SPICED VEGETABLE AND CASHEW NUT PILAU

Although the ingredients list is quite long, this is actually very quick and easy to make. My favourite accompaniments are fresh chutney, mango chutney and poppadums. I've given quantities to serve two, but for four just double everything except the oil. You can use brown or white basmati rice – white cooks more quickly.

2 tbls oil	200g / 7oz basmati rice
1 onion, peeled and chopped	small piece of cinnamon stick
1 carrot, finely sliced	¼ tsp turmeric
1 leek, cleaned and sliced	1 bay leaf
1 garlic clove, crushed	50g / 2oz cashew nuts
6 cardamom pods	salt and freshly ground black pepper
1 tsp cumin seeds	

1 Heat the oil in a saucepan, then put in the onion and carrot, cover and cook for 5 minutes. Stir in the leek, garlic, cardamom and cumin, crushing the cardomom pods against the pan with a wooden spoon. Cover and cook for another 5–10 minutes, stirring occasionally, until the vegetables are tender.

2 Meanwhile, wash the rice in a sieve under the cold tap then put it into a saucepan with the cinnamon stick, turmeric, bay leaf and 450ml/¾ pint of water. Bring to the boil, then cover, turn the heat right down and leave it to cook very gently for 10–12 minutes.

3 Heat the grill. Spread out the cashew nuts on a grill pan and grill for 1–2 minutes, until they are golden brown, turning them to brown both sides. Remove from the grill and leave on one side.

4 Fork the rice gently, then combine it with the vegetable mixture, stirring gently with the fork and adding some salt and pepper. Stir the cashew nuts into the mixture just before you serve it.
SERVES 2

RICE WITH TOMATOES, SWEETCORN AND CHILLI

The best rice to use for this is either ordinary white long grain rice or brown basmati, although you could use quick-cook brown long grain rice instead.

1 tbls oil	1 bay leaf
1 onion, peeled and chopped	125g / 4oz frozen sweetcorn
1 fresh chilli	125g / 4oz frozen peas
1 garlic clove, crushed	salt and freshly ground black pepper
200g / 7oz rice	2 tbls chopped fresh parsley
1 × 225g / 8oz can tomatoes	

1 Heat the oil in a large saucepan, then put in the onion, cover and cook for 5 minutes.

2 Halve, de-seed and chop the chilli, being careful not to get the juice anywhere near your face, and washing your hands well afterwards. Add the chilli and the garlic to the pan and stir well.

3 Add the rice, tomatoes, bay leaf and 450ml/¾ pint of water to the pan. Bring to the boil, then turn down the heat, cover and leave to cook very gently for 20 minutes for brown basmati rice, 15–20 minutes for long grain white rice or 25 minutes for quick-cook brown rice.

4 Cook the frozen sweetcorn and peas together in a little boiling water for 2 minutes then drain and add them to the rice mixture, along with some salt, pepper and the parsley. Stir gently with a fork and serve as soon as possible.
SERVES 2

WARM RICE SALAD

This looks fresh and pretty and is made with a delicious honey and garlic dressing; you can leave out the oil if you want a lighter result.

200g / 7oz basmati rice
1 garlic clove, crushed
1 tbls honey
1 tbls vinegar
1 tbls olive oil
salt and freshly
  ground black pepper

225g / 8oz cherry
  tomatoes
4 tbls chopped fresh
  chives
4 tbls chopped fresh
  mint

1. Wash the rice in a sieve under the cold tap then put it into a saucepan with 450ml/¾ pint of water. Bring to the boil, then cover, turn the heat right down and leave it to cook gently for 10–12 minutes. Turn off the heat and let the rice stand, covered, for a further 10 minutes, if there is time.

2. While the rice is cooking, make the dressing: put the garlic, honey, vinegar, olive oil and some salt and pepper into a large bowl and mix well.

3. Wash and slice the cherry tomatoes. Put the rice into the bowl with the dressing, add the cherry tomatoes and herbs then stir gently with a fork. Check the seasoning, then serve while still warm.

SERVES 2–3

EGG AND COCONUT CURRY

75g / 3oz desiccated
  coconut
2 eggs
175g / 6oz brown or
  white basmati rice
½ cinnamon stick
4 cloves
4 cardamom pods
salt and freshly
  ground black pepper

25g / 1oz butter
1 onion, peeled and
  chopped
1 garlic clove, crushed
2 tsp medium curry
  powder
25g / 1oz plain flour
25g / 1oz sultanas
1 tbls lemon juice

1. Put the coconut in a bowl and cover with 450ml/¾ pint of boiling water. Leave to infuse.

2. Hard-boil the eggs by simmering them in a pan of boiling water for 7–10 minutes. Then drain them, cover with cold water and leave to cool.

3. Wash the rice in a sieve under the cold tap. Put it in a saucepan with 350ml/12fl oz of water, the cinnamon stick, cloves and cardamom, crushing the cardamom pods against the side of the pan with a wooden spoon. Add a good pinch of salt and bring to the boil.

4. Turn the heat down very low and leave the rice to cook until it is tender and all the water has been absorbed, 20 minutes for brown rice, 10–12 minutes for white rice. Then turn off the heat and leave it to stand, still covered, for 10 minutes.

5. Meanwhile, melt the butter in a pan and gently cook the onion and garlic for 5 minutes. Strain the coconut through a sieve, pressing it against the sieve to extract as much liquid as possible. Discard the coconut but keep the liquid.

6. Stir the curry powder into the onion mixture, then add the flour and stir for 1–2 minutes until it froths. Pour in the strained coconut water, stirring until it thickens. Add the sultanas, then let it simmer very gently for 7–10 minutes.

7. Make sure the rice is still hot and check the seasoning; reheat it gently if necessary. Shell and slice the hard-boiled eggs and then add them to the sauce with the lemon juice and salt and pepper to taste. Fluff up the rice with a fork and serve with the curry.

SERVES 2

VARIATIONS

1 CHEESE CURRY

Cut 125g/4oz cheese – haloumi if you want one that keeps its shape, or good old Cheddar for a 'melting' result – into smallish cubes and stir them into the sauce instead of the eggs. Heat gently until the cheese has warmed through, then serve.

2 BUTTERBEAN OR SOYA BEAN CURRY

Add 225g/8oz canned beans to the sauce instead of the eggs and cook gently until heated through.

This is a simple English-style curry rather than an authentically spiced Indian one, and I think it makes a pleasant change. Using a medium curry powder will produce a mild curry here; you can adjust the heat according to the type and amount of curry powder you use.

ALL-SEASONS MUSHROOM RISOTTO

My favourite risotto is this rich-tasting mushroom one, with extra flavour coming from the porcini. Chestnut mushrooms are good if you can get them, because they retain their firm texture and don't produce much liquid.

Although if pushed you can use an ordinary long grain rice, Arborio or risotto rice (which is now quite widely available) is best because it cooks to exactly the right creamy consistency, with the grains tender but slightly chewy.

1 × 10g / ¼ oz packet
  porcini mushrooms
1 bay leaf
3 tbls olive oil
50g / 2oz butter
1 onion, peeled and
  chopped
350g / 12oz chestnut
  mushrooms or
  button mushrooms
2 garlic cloves,
  crushed

350g / 12oz Arborio or
  other risotto rice
salt and freshly
  ground black pepper
chopped fresh parsley,
  preferably flat-leaf
50g / 2oz fresh
  Parmesan cheese, cut
  into thin slivers

1 Put the porcini into a saucepan with the bay leaf and 1.5 litres/2½ pints of boiling water. Let it simmer while you prepare the other ingredients.

2 Heat the olive oil and half the butter in a large saucepan, then put in the onion, cover and cook for about 5 minutes, until soft but not browned.

3 Slice the fresh mushrooms and add to the onion with the garlic and rice. Stir for 2–3 minutes, until the rice is coated with the buttery juices.

4 Add a ladleful of the simmering water from the pan containing the porcini and stir well; once it has been absorbed, add another. Keep the water in the porcini pan simmering away and continue to add it to the risotto a ladleful at a time as each addition is absorbed, stirring the risotto constantly.

5 Fish out the porcini from the pan, chop them up and add them to the risotto. Stop adding water once the rice is tender but not soggy – *al dente*, in fact. This will be after about 20 minutes and you will probably have used all the water.

6 Stir in the rest of the butter and season to taste with salt and pepper. Serve immediately, scattered with the parsley and slivers of Parmesan.
SERVES 4

QUICK MICROWAVE RISOTTO

It's blissfully easy to make a risotto in the microwave and the results are wonderful. This method was developed by the American cookery writer Barbara Kafka, and works like a dream.

25g / 1oz butter
1 tbls olive oil
1 onion, peeled and
  chopped
3 garlic cloves,
  crushed

175g / 6oz Arborio or
  other risotto rice
50g / 2oz fresh
  Parmesan cheese
salt and freshly
  ground black pepper

1 Put the butter and oil into a deep, microwave-proof casserole, put into the microwave and cook, uncovered, on high for 2 minutes.

2 Add the onion and garlic and stir to coat them in the butter and oil. Cook, uncovered, on high, for 4 minutes.

3 Add the rice, stir, then cook, uncovered, on high for 4 minutes.

4 Pour in 750ml/1¼ pints of boiling water. Cook, uncovered, on high for 9 minutes. Stir well, then cook for 9 minutes more.

5 Remove from the microwave. Leave the risotto to stand, uncovered, for 5 minutes, so the rice absorbs the rest of the liquid; stir it several times. Flake the Parmesan with a potato peeler or a sharp knife then stir this in, together with salt and pepper to taste. Serve immediately.
SERVES 2

OPPOSITE: *All-Seasons Mushroom Risotto*

BULGUR, COUSCOUS & POLENTA
✳

BULGUR AND CHEESE PILAU

Bulgur wheat is crushed and pre-cooked so it is quick to prepare. You can serve it as an accompaniment, like rice, or you can stir in some extra ingredients and turn it into a main course, as in this recipe.

1 tbls olive oil
15g / ½ oz butter
1 onion, peeled and chopped
1 red pepper, de-seeded and chopped
2 garlic cloves, crushed
225g / 8oz bulgur wheat

50g / 2oz raisins
salt and freshly ground black pepper
50g / 2oz almonds
100g / 3½oz Gruyère cheese
2 tbls chopped fresh parsley

Serve this pilau with a salad of green leaves, herbs, a little finely sliced onion, and a light lemon and olive oil dressing. A soured cream sauce is a luxurious finishing touch (see page 77).

1 Heat the oil and butter in a large saucepan and put in the onion and red pepper; stir, then cover and leave to cook gently for 5–10 minutes. Add the garlic, then boil some water in a kettle.

2 Add the bulgur wheat and raisins to the onion and pepper mixture, stirring well so that the wheat gets coated with the butter and oil, then pour in 600ml/1 pint of boiling water and add a good teaspoonful of salt. Bring to the boil, then cover and leave to cook gently for 15 minutes.

3 Meanwhile put the almonds into a small saucepan, cover with water and bring to the boil. Boil for 1–2 minutes, then drain and slip off the skins with your fingers.

4 Heat the grill. Cut the almonds lengthwise with a sharp knife to make long slivers. Spread these out on a grill pan and grill them for 1–2 minutes, until golden brown.

5 Cut the Gruyère cheese into 6 mm/½ inch dice. Add them to the bulgur wheat, together with cheese and parsley, forking them through gently. Check the seasoning, then serve.
SERVES 4

BRIGHTLY COLOURED TABBOULEH

Here's a deliciously inauthentic version of this famous salad: it isn't left to stand for hours and it's a riot of colour. It tastes wonderful and doesn't need any accompaniments.

175g / 6oz bulgur wheat
1 red pepper
1 yellow pepper
1 garlic clove, crushed
juice of ½ lemon
1–2 tbls olive oil
salt and freshly ground black pepper

2–3 tomatoes
4 spring onions
1 small avocado
1 small head of radicchio
8 sprigs of flat-leaf parsley

1 Boil some water in a kettle and set the grill on high. Put the bulgur wheat into a large bowl then cover with 350ml/12fl oz of boiling water. Leave on one side to swell.

2 Cut the peppers into quarters, place them cut-side down on a grill pan and grill for 10 minutes or until the skins have blistered and charred in places. Remove from the grill and cover with a damp cloth.

3 Meanwhile, put the garlic into a bowl with the lemon juice, olive oil and some salt and pepper.

4 Wash and chop the tomatoes and trim and chop the spring onions. Peel, stone and chop the avocado. Wash and roughly tear the radicchio and parsley. Add all these to the garlic.

5 Peel the peppers, pulling off the skin with a sharp knife; discard the seeds and stalks, then cut the flesh into strips and add to the other salad ingredients in the bowl.

6 Fork through the bulgur wheat then add this to the salad and mix gently to distribute all the ingredients well, adding some salt and pepper to taste as you do so.
SERVES 2 AS A MAIN COURSE, 4–6 AS AN ACCOMPANIMENT

VEGETABLE COUSCOUS

This is a quick way with couscous that may not result in every grain being immaculately separate, but who cares? It tastes good, and it doesn't need any accompaniment except perhaps a glass of spicy wine.

1 fennel bulb	225g / 8oz tomatoes
225g / 8oz carrots	225g / 8oz courgettes
2 tbls olive oil	225g / 8oz couscous
1 onion, peeled and chopped	15g / ½oz butter
1 tbls coriander seeds	1–2 tbls chopped fresh parsley
1 garlic clove, crushed	

1. Trim off any green leafy bits from the fennel, then pare away any tough outer layers using a potato peeler or sharp knife. Slice the fennel; scrape and slice the carrots.

2. Heat the oil in a large pan and put in the fennel, carrots and onion. Cover and leave to cook gently, with a lid on the pan, for 10 minutes.

3. Meanwhile, crush the coriander seeds in a pestle and mortar or with a wooden spoon. Then add these to the vegetables, along with the garlic.

4. Put the tomatoes into a bowl, cover with boiling water and leave for a few seconds until the skins split. Drain, cover with cold water and slip off the skins with a sharp knife. De-seed and chop the tomatoes and add them to the pan.

5. Wash, trim and slice the courgettes and add these to the pan, too. If the vegetables show any signs of sticking, add 1–2 tablespoons of water. Cover and cook for 5 minutes or until the courgettes are tender.

6. Meanwhile, prepare the couscous. Put 300ml/½ pint of water into a saucepan and bring to the boil. Sprinkle in the couscous, then remove the pan from the heat and leave for 2 minutes. Add the butter and a little seasoning, put the pan back on the stove and heat gently, stirring with a fork, for 3 minutes.

7. By this time the vegetables should all be tender. Check the seasoning, sprinkle with the parsley and serve with the couscous.

SERVES 2–3

SWEET COUSCOUS WITH APRICOTS

This is a very adaptable dish. While I really created it as a pudding it also makes a delicious brunch recipe, and can even be served as a salad if you put it on a base of lettuce. If you try it, you'll see what I mean. Some thick Greek yogurt goes particularly well with it, however you serve it.

50g / 2oz ready-to-eat dried apricots	½ tsp cinnamon
50g / 2oz raisins	1 tbls clear honey
25g / 1oz creamed coconut	125g / 4oz couscous
	25g / 1oz flaked almonds

1. Chop the apricots roughly then put them into a saucepan with the raisins and enough water just to cover. Bring to the boil then cover and leave to simmer gently while you prepare the couscous.

2. Cut the creamed coconut into flakes or tiny cubes then put it into a saucepan with the cinnamon, honey and 300ml/½ pint of water. Heat gently until the water comes to the boil and the coconut cream has melted, then pour in the couscous. Cover and remove from the heat.

3. Heat the grill. Spread the almonds out on a grill pan and grill for 1–2 minutes, until they are golden brown.

4. Stir the couscous gently with a fork to separate the grains. Drain the apricots and raisins, or boil rapidly to evaporate the water, if you prefer. Add the apricots and raisins to the couscous, along with the toasted flaked almonds.

SERVES 2–4

Creamed coconut can be bought in a block and will keep for ages in the fridge after opening.

INSTANT POLENTA WITH GRILLED VEGETABLES

1 tsp salt
75g / 3oz instant
 polenta
1 large red onion
1 large fennel bulb
2 beefsteak tomatoes

225g / 8oz large flat
 mushrooms
olive oil
1 or 2 sprigs of
 rosemary

1 Put 300ml/½ pint of water and the salt into a medium non-stick saucepan and bring to the boil, then sprinkle the polenta in and stir until smooth. Let the mixture cook gently for 4–5 minutes, until it has thickened, then tip it on to a large flat plate and quickly spread it out so that it is about 1 cm/½ inch thick. Leave to cool while you prepare the vegetables. Set the grill to high.

2 Bring 5 cm/2 inches of water to the boil in another pan for the onion and fennel. Peel the onion. Trim the fennel by removing any tough leaves or pieces of stem but leaving enough stem to hold the leaves together at the base. Cut the fennel and the onion down first into halves, then into quarters and eighths.

3 Cook the onion and fennel in the boiling water for about 6–8 minutes or until they are just tender without being at all soggy. Drain well and dry on kitchen paper.

4 Thickly slice the tomatoes; wash and trim the mushrooms.

5 Brush all the vegetables with olive oil, then arrange them on a grill pan, sprinkle with the leaves from the rosemary sprigs and grill for about 15 minutes or until lightly charred on both sides, turning as necessary.

6 Meanwhile, cut the polenta into triangles and fry them in olive oil in a frying pan for about 4–5 minutes per side, until crisp and lightly browned. Drain the polenta on kitchen paper and serve with the vegetables.

SERVES 2

OPPOSITE: **Instant Polenta with Grilled Vegetables**

VARIATION

POLENTA WITH GARLIC MAYONNAISE AND SALAD

Make the polenta as described above. Serve the fried polenta with a lettuce, tomato and spring onion salad and some garlic mayonnaise made by stirring 1 garlic clove, crushed, into 4 tablespoons of mayonnaise, or a mixture of mayonnaise and yogurt.

OLIVE POLENTA WITH TOMATO SAUCE

1 tsp salt
75g / 3oz instant
 polenta
50g / 2oz olives, green
 or black or a mixture
olive oil
1 onion, peeled and
 chopped

1 garlic clove, crushed
1 × 400g / 14oz can
 tomatoes
salt and freshly
 ground black pepper

1 Put 300ml/½ pint of water and the salt into a medium non-stick saucepan and bring to the boil, then sprinkle the polenta in and stir until smooth. Cook gently for 4–5 minutes, until it has thickened.

2 Stone the olives and stir them into the cooked polenta then tip it on to a large flat plate and quickly spread it out so that it is about 1 cm/½ inch thick. Leave to cool while you prepare the sauce.

3 Heat 1 tablespoon of oil in a pan then add the onion, cover and cook gently for 10 minutes. Add the garlic and cook for 1–2 minutes, then stir in the tomatoes together with their juice, breaking them up with a wooden spoon. Simmer for 10–15 minutes until the excess liquid has evaporated.

4 Meanwhile, cut the polenta into pieces and fry in olive oil for about 4–5 minutes per side until crisp and lightly browned. Drain on kitchen paper.

5 Season the sauce with salt and pepper and serve with the polenta.

SERVES 2

I have recently discovered instant polenta, which I find excellent – it brings polenta into the fast-food category and I prefer the flavour to that of traditional slow-cooking polenta. Serve it with grilled vegetables for a meal that really brings the Mediterranean sunshine with it.

The olives give this a pleasant salty tang. Serve with a refreshing side salad.

NUTS
— ✳ —

LITTLE NUT CROQUETTES WITH CAPER SAUCE

Serve these crunchy nut croquettes with a quick-cooking vegetable such as mangetout or green beans, or with a crisp green salad or a tomato, avocado and basil salad. Some mashed potatoes go well with them, too, for a more substantial meal.

50g / 2oz butter
4 tbls plain flour
1 bay leaf
600ml / 1 pint milk
1 large onion, peeled and finely chopped
1 tbls olive oil
100g / 3½oz bread
100g / 3½oz cashew nuts
100g / 3½oz pecan nuts
salt and freshly ground black pepper
3 tbls capers
2 tsp wine vinegar
2 tbls chopped fresh chives
oil for deep-frying

1. Melt the butter in a medium saucepan and stir in the flour. Cook for 1–2 minutes, stirring, then add the bay leaf and half the milk; bring to a simmer and stir until very thick. Put half the mixture in a bowl and set aside. Then stir the remaining milk into the pan, beating hard until smooth. Leave the sauce to simmer very gently for a few minutes.
2. Meanwhile, gently fry the onion in the oil for 5–10 minutes, until lightly browned.
3. Break the bread into chunks and put it into a food processor with the cashew nuts and pecans; whizz until they are all finely chopped.
4. Add the reserved thick sauce to the onion, along with the nuts and breadcrumbs and some salt and pepper to taste. Add a little water, if necessary, for a firm but soft and pliable consistency. Form the mixture into 20 balls roughly the size of walnuts.
5. Add the capers, vinegar, chives and some salt and pepper to the sauce, then keep warm.
6. Heat some oil for deep-frying in a saucepan, wok or deep-fryer. Test the temperature by dipping a wooden chopstick or the handle of a wooden spoon into it: the oil should immediately form bubbles around it. Put in the croquettes and fry for 4–5 minutes, until brown and crisp. Drain on kitchen paper and serve at once, in a pool of the sauce.
SERVES 4

CHESTNUT AND MUSHROOM CASSEROLE

This goes well with mashed potatoes or, better still, baked potatoes – the timing of these will fit in if you allow the longer cooking time for the casserole.

5 outer stems from 1 head of celery
2 large carrots
2 large leeks
2 tbls olive oil
1 large onion, peeled and chopped
225g / 8oz field or button mushrooms
2 garlic cloves, crushed
1 × 250g / 9oz can whole chestnuts
2 tbls plain flour
good sprig of thyme
150ml / 5fl oz red wine
1 tsp vegetable stock concentrate
2 tbls soy sauce
salt and freshly ground black pepper
chopped fresh parsley

1. Wash, trim and slice the celery. Put it into a saucepan with 600ml/1 pint of water and bring to the boil. Scrape and slice the carrots; wash, trim and slice the leeks. Add all these to the pan.
2. While the vegetables simmer away, heat the oil in another pan and fry the onion for 5 minutes. Slice the mushrooms and add to the onion, along with the garlic. Stir and cook for 5 minutes.
3. Add the chestnuts to the onion mixture, then stir in the flour and cook for 2 minutes. Tip in the vegetables from the other pan, with their water.
4. Add the thyme, wine, stock concentrate, soy sauce and seasoning. Simmer gently until all the vegetables are tender. This may take only 10 minutes, but if you have time to cook it for longer – up to 45 minutes – the flavours will improve. Serve sprinkled with chopped parsley.
SERVES 4

OPPOSITE: *(top) Chestnut and Mushroom Casserole and (bottom) Little Nut Croquettes with Caper Sauce*

CHESTNUTS WITH SAVOY CABBAGE AND SAGE

This is a particularly warming and delicious dish for the autumn and winter. Do use Savoy cabbage if you can get it because its flavour is the best, although other types of cabbage can be used as well. I like this as a main course, served with some light, creamy mashed potatoes.

Different types of nuts can be used in the pâté, but they are best if they are roasted first. This can be done under the grill or in the oven at 180°C/350°F/ Gas Mark 4 for about 20 minutes, until golden brown. In the case of hazelnuts, rub off the skins in a soft cloth. For speed, use ready-roasted nuts.

25g / 1oz butter
1 onion, peeled and
  sliced
1 garlic clove, crushed
½ Savoy cabbage,
  about 225g / 8oz after
  trimming

1 × 250g / 9oz can
  whole chestnuts
2–3 sprigs of sage
salt and freshly
  ground black pepper

[1] Melt the butter in a medium saucepan and put in the onion; stir, then cover and cook gently for 5 minutes. Add the garlic, then cover and cook for 1–2 minutes longer.
[2] Meanwhile, wash and coarsely shred the cabbage, then cook it in 1 cm/½ inch of boiling water for about 7 minutes or until just tender.
[3] Add the chestnuts to the onion mixture in the pan, mashing them a bit to break them up. Heat gently until the chestnuts are warmed through.
[4] Drain the cabbage thoroughly and add it to the chestnut mixture. Tear in the sage leaves, then season everything well with salt and pepper and serve immediately.
SERVES 2

NUT PATE WITH DATE AND MINT CHUTNEY

This is one of the nicest nut pâté mixtures I know. It's equally good hot or cold, with a cooked vegetable such as green beans or a salad. The chutney makes a delicious accompaniment, but if you don't have time to prepare it the pâté is equally good without it.

150g / 5oz low-fat
  garlic and herb soft
  cheese
150g / 5oz roasted
  cashew nuts
dash of Tabasco or
  hot pepper sauce
  (optional)
50g / 2oz dried
  breadcrumbs
  (optional)

FOR THE CHUTNEY
125g / 4oz dates
1 small onion, peeled
  and chopped
1 tbls wine vinegar
2 tbls chopped fresh
  mint
pinch of cayenne
  pepper
salt and freshly
  ground black pepper

[1] Make the chutney first to allow time for the flavours to develop: chop the dates then put them into a saucepan with the onion, vinegar and 3 tablespoons of water. Cover and cook gently for about 5 minutes, until both have softened and the mixture is no longer liquid.
[2] Remove from the heat and add the chopped mint, cayenne pepper and some salt and pepper to taste. Transfer to a bowl and leave on one side.
[3] Next make the pâté: put the cheese into a bowl and mash until soft and creamy. Grind the nuts in a food processor or with a rotary hand grater.
[4] Stir the nuts into the cheese to form a mixture that is soft but will hold its shape. Add the Tabasco, if you wish, and season with salt and pepper.
[5] Form the pâté into a log shape then coat it all over with the breadcrumbs, if you are using these.
[6] Serve the pâté as it is (it can be chilled until needed, in which case it will firm up a bit more), or put it under a moderate grill and grill for about 3 minutes each on the top, bottom and sides, until crisp and brown and heated right through. Cut into 6 slices and serve with the date and mint chutney, if you're having this.
SERVES 2

CELERY ALMONDINE

This simple dish consists of celery in a creamy sauce with a base and topping of flaked almonds. Serve as a starter or an accompaniment, or with some boiled new potatoes for a light and unusual main course.

1 head of celery or 2 celery hearts
1 bay leaf
25g / 1oz butter
1 onion, peeled and chopped
100g / 3½ oz flaked almonds
a little milk (optional)
25g / 1oz plain flour
2 tbls cream
salt and freshly ground black pepper

1   Wash and trim the celery, removing any damaged or tough stems, then chop it quite finely: do this by cutting down the length of each stem several times to produce long, thin strips then cutting across to produce little dice.

2   Put the celery into a saucepan with the bay leaf and water just to cover, then bring to the boil, cover and simmer for about 15 minutes or until the celery is very tender.

3   Meanwhile, melt the butter in a saucepan, add the onion and cook gently, covered, for about 5 minutes or until softened.

4   Heat the grill. Spread half the almonds out on a grill pan and grill for 1–2 minutes, until golden brown. Remove from the grill, leaving the grill on.

5   Drain the celery, reserving the liquid and making it up to 300ml/½ pint if necessary with some water or a little milk.

6   Stir the flour into the onion and cook for 1–2 minutes. Then add the celery liquid, stirring all the time. Simmer gently over a very low heat for about 5 minutes. Add the celery and continue to cook gently until the celery is heated through.

7   Scatter the toasted almonds evenly over the base of a shallow gratin dish. Stir the cream into the celery mixture, season with salt and pepper, then spoon it into the dish on top of the almonds. Sprinkle the remaining, untoasted, almonds on top and put it under the grill until the almonds are golden brown and everything is piping hot.

SERVES 2 AS A MAIN COURSE

CHESTNUT FOOL

1 × 250g / 9oz can unsweetened chestnut purée
50g / 2oz icing sugar
2 tbls brandy or Armagnac
300ml / ½ pint whipping cream
***marrons glacés** and/or grated chocolate to decorate*

1   Put the chestnut purée into a large bowl with the icing sugar and brandy or Armagnac and beat it until it is smooth.

2   Whisk the cream until it is thick but not standing in peaks, then fold it into the chestnut mixture.

3   Spoon the mixture into small glasses and decorate with *marrons glacés* or grated chocolate (or both). Chill until needed.

SERVES 6

ALMOND AND CHOCOLATE SLICES

200g / 7oz good-quality milk chocolate
100g / 3½ oz flaked almonds
100g / 3½ oz raisins
75g / 3oz cornflakes

1   Break the chocolate into pieces and put it into a large bowl set over a pan of steaming water. Leave until the chocolate has melted. Meanwhile, line a 20 cm/8 inch square cake tin with non-stick paper.

2   Remove the bowl of chocolate from the pan. Add the flaked almonds and raisins then add the cornflakes, crushing them with your hands as you do so; they need to be slightly powdery.

3   Mix thoroughly, then spoon the mixture into the tin, spreading it right into the corners and pressing it down well. Put the tin in the fridge or even the freezer if you are very rushed. It will set in about 10–15 minutes and can then be turned out, stripped of the paper, and cut into pieces.

MAKES 9

This pudding can be whizzed up at a moment's notice. Stand the can of chestnut purée on a radiator or in a pan of very hot water for a few minutes before using it, if there's time, because then it will be soft and easy to mix.

This is a variation on the well-known cornflakes-and-chocolate crunchies adored by children. It's a useful recipe if you need to produce home-made biscuits in a hurry.

VEGETABLES

Vegetables are excellent fast foods and make the basis of hundreds of speedy dishes. Most are quick to cook or can be served raw, and now that you can buy many of them ready washed the preparation time is even quicker. They can be made into wonderful main courses such as Provençal Potatoes, Broccoli with Cashew Sauce or Grilled Mediterranean Vegetables with Mozzarella; comforting soups, including Green Pea and Mint and Creamy Onion; or salads such as Thai Cabbage Salad or Italian Country Salad; vegetables are so versatile that there's plenty of scope for experiment.

SOUPS & TOP-OF-THE-STOVE DISHES

GREEN PEA AND MINT SOUP

If you're looking for a quick soup this one is hard to beat. Although it can be made all year round, it has a refreshing summery flavour.

15g / ½oz butter
1 onion, peeled and
 chopped
125g / 4oz potato, diced
450g / 1lb frozen petits
 pois

4–5 sprigs of mint
salt and freshly ground
 black pepper
1–2 tbls lemon juice

1. Melt the butter in a large saucepan and gently fry the onion and potato for about 10 minutes.
2. Add the petit pois, the leaves from the mint sprigs, and 1 litre/1¾ pints of water. Bring to the boil, then simmer gently for 10–15 minutes or until the potato and onion are tender.
3. Liquidize the soup, then pour it through a sieve back into the pan. Thin with a little water if you like, then reheat gently. Season well with salt and pepper and a good squeeze of lemon juice.
SERVES 4

QUICK VEGETABLE SOUP

Although this soup is very quick to make, the vegetables are cooked slowly in oil initially, which really helps them to release their flavour.

225g / 8oz carrots
225g / 8oz parsnips
225g / 8oz leeks
1 tbls light olive oil
1 × 400g / 14oz can
 tomatoes

2 tbls chopped fresh
 parsley
salt and freshly
 ground black pepper

1. Scrape the carrots and cut them into tiny dice. Peel the parsnips and dice them in the same way then trim the leeks and slice them finely.
2. Heat the oil in a large saucepan and put in the vegetables. Cover and cook gently for 10 minutes, then add the tomatoes with their juice and 600ml/ 1 pint of water. Bring to the boil then reduce the heat and simmer for about 15 minutes, until tender.
3. Add the parsley, season with salt and pepper, then serve in warmed bowls.
SERVES 2–3

CREAMY ONION SOUP

700g / 1½lb potatoes
700g / 1½lb onions
25g / 1oz butter
3–4 tbls single cream
 (optional)

salt and freshly
 ground black pepper
freshly grated nutmeg

1. Peel and dice the potatoes and put them into a saucepan with 450 ml/¾ pint of water. Bring to the boil, then cover and simmer for 15–20 minutes, until very tender. Meanwhile, peel the onions and slice them into half-circles.
2. Melt the butter in another saucepan and put in the onions. Cover and cook over a gentle heat until tender. This will take about 15 minutes and they'll need stirring from time to time to prevent sticking.
3. When the potatoes are done, either mash them very thoroughly in their water or, which is easier, whizz them to a purée in a food processor then return them to the pan.
4. Tip the onions and their liquid into the potato purée and add the cream, if you're using this. Thin the soup with a little more water, reheat gently, then season with salt, pepper and freshly grated nutmeg.
SERVES 4

This is a very adaptable vegetable soup: throw in a handful of small pasta and add a little extra liquid 10 minutes before serving to make it more substantial; and/or add a can of haricot or cannellini beans. For a Mediterranean flavour, stir in a couple of spoonfuls of pesto just before you serve it. Eat it as it is, or with grated cheese on top. Some country-style bread goes well with it, too.

ROOT VEGETABLES STEWED IN OIL AND BUTTER

A warming dish for winter and one of my favourite ways of cooking root vegetables. You can use any combination you like: celeriac, Jerusalem artichokes, turnips and kohlrabi are all good. Serve this as a main course, with some coarse country-style bread.

225g / 8oz onions
225g / 8oz carrots
225g / 8oz parsnips
225g / 8oz sweet
  potatoes
2 tbls olive oil

25g / 1oz butter
salt and freshly
  ground black pepper
a little chopped fresh
  parsley, if available

1 Peel and chop the onions; scrape the carrots and slice them thinly. Peel and slice the parsnips and sweet potatoes – these can be in slightly bigger pieces.

2 Heat the oil and butter in a large saucepan and put in the vegetables. Cook very gently, with a lid on the pan, for 15–20 minutes or until tender.

3 Season with salt and pepper and scatter with a little chopped parsley, if available.

SERVES 2

VARIATION

LEEKS AND POTATOES STEWED IN OIL AND BUTTER

Substitute 450g/1lb potatoes and 450g/1lb leeks for the root vegetables. Peel the potatoes and cut them into quite chunky slices; wash the leeks and slice them fairly thickly. Then proceed as above.

BROCCOLI WITH CASHEW SAUCE

Creamy and lightly spiced, this is delicious served with plain rice and some Indian bread.

1 tbls oil
1 onion, peeled and
  chopped
1 cinnamon stick,
  broken
small knob of fresh
  ginger root
1 garlic clove, crushed
6–8 cardamom pods

½ tsp turmeric
100g / 3½ oz cashew
  nuts
salt and freshly
  ground black pepper
1–2 tbls lemon juice
  (optional)
450g / 1lb broccoli

1 Heat the oil in a medium saucepan, add the onion and the cinnamon stick then cover and cook gently for 5 minutes, until the onion has softened. Grate the ginger on the fine side of a grater, add the ginger and the garlic to the onion, cover again and cook for 2–3 minutes.

2 Crush the cardamom so that the seeds come out of the pods; discard the pods and crush the seeds a bit. Stir these into the onion along with the turmeric and cook for 1–2 minutes longer.

3 Take the cinnamon out of the pan but don't throw it away. Tip the onion mixture into a food processor and add the cashew nuts and 300ml/ ½ pint of water. Whizz thoroughly until creamy.

4 Tip the mixture back into the pan and add the cinnamon stick again. Season with salt and pepper, sharpen with a little lemon juice if necessary, then reheat the sauce gently and keep it warm while you prepare the broccoli.

5 Wash the broccoli and divide it into florets. Peel the stems thickly to remove any tough skin, then slice them into rounds or matchsticks. Cook the broccoli in 2.5 cm/1 inch of boiling water for about 3–4 minutes, until tender; don't let it get soggy. Drain immediately and season lightly.

6 You can mix the broccoli into the cashew sauce or pour a little of the sauce on to warmed serving plates, top with the broccoli and pour the remaining sauce on top – this looks more attractive.

SERVES 2

Many other vegetables can be substituted for the broccoli: try carrots, green beans, cauliflower, pumpkin, okra, or a mixture.

LEMONY SPRING VEGETABLES

Tender spring vegetables and early herbs are so delicious and welcome when they arrive that I like to serve them on their own as a main course. You can use whatever vegetables are available, choosing contrasting colours and flavours.

225g / 8oz tiny new
  potatoes
225g / 8oz baby carrots
225g / 8oz young green
  beans, or broad beans
  still in their pods
225g / 8oz baby
  turnips or fennel

15–25g / ½–1oz butter
chopped fresh herbs,
  such as mint, parsley,
  chives, tarragon or
  chervil
squeeze of lemon juice
salt and freshly
  ground black pepper

1 Bring 5 cm/2 inches of water to the boil in a large pan. Meanwhile, clean and trim the vegetables as necessary.

2 Put the vegetables into the boiling water, adding them according to the time they will take to cook: about 10 minutes for the potatoes and carrots; 6–8 minutes for the turnips and fennel; and 2 minutes for the beans. Cook until just tender.

3 Drain the vegetables, add the butter, herbs, lemon juice and seasoning, then serve at once.
SERVES 2

PROVENCAL POTATOES

This is good served with green salad or some baby spinach – for speed, buy spinach ready washed and microwave it in the packet, or cook it without water in a pan for a few minutes until just wilted.

1 onion, peeled and
  chopped
1 tbls olive oil
1 garlic clove, crushed
1 × 400g / 14oz can
  tomatoes
350g / 12oz potatoes
2 sun-dried tomatoes
  in oil, drained

50g / 2oz Kalamata
  olives
salt and freshly
  ground black pepper
shavings of fresh
  Parmesan cheese
  (optional)

1 Fry the onion in the oil for 5 minutes, then add the garlic and the canned tomatoes, breaking the tomatoes up with a wooden spoon. Bring to the boil and simmer for 10–15 minutes, until very thick.

2 Meanwhile, bring 5 cm/2 inches of water to the boil for the potatoes. Peel the potatoes then cut them into 6 mm/¼ inch thick slices. Add to the pan, cover and simmer for 7–10 minutes, until tender but not breaking up, then drain.

3 Chop the sun-dried tomatoes and add to the sauce along with half the olives. Season, then mix together the sauce and the potatoes, top with the remaining olives and serve immediately. Or top with Parmesan cheese, brown under the grill, then garnish with the remaining olives and serve.
SERVES 2

COLCANNON

700g / 1½ lb potatoes
700g / 1½ lb kale or
  dark cabbage
2 leeks

125ml / 4fl oz milk or
  single cream
50g / 2oz butter
salt and freshly
  ground black pepper

1 Peel and dice the potatoes then boil for 15–20 minutes, until tender.

2 Meanwhile, wash the kale or cabbage, remove any tough stems and shred the rest coarsely. Cook, covered, in 1 cm/½ inch of boiling water for 15–20 minutes: it needs cooking for longer than usual.

3 Clean and trim the leeks then slice them quite finely. Put them into a saucepan with the milk or cream and simmer gently for 5–6 minutes, until tender. Put the butter into a small bowl and set it on top of the pan of leeks to melt the butter.

4 Drain the kale or cabbage and quickly chop it. Put it back in the pan to keep warm.

5 Drain the potatoes and mash with the leeks and milk or cream. Mix in the kale and season well. Transfer the mixture to heated plates, make a well in the centre and pour the melted butter into it.
SERVES 4

OPPOSITE: *(left) Quick Vegetable Soup, page 98, (right) Lemony Spring Vegetables, (bottom) Provençal Potatoes*

GRATINS & GRILLS
✳

CHEESY VEGETABLE GRATIN

This works best if you use a big shallow gratin dish so that you end up with quite a thin layer of vegetables and lots of lovely, golden cheesy topping. You can use a variety of different vegetables; choose ones that take about the same time to cook, or add them to the boiling water in succession, according to their cooking time.

Balsamic vinegar has a wonderful sweet, mellow flavour and comes in a wide price range, depending on how long it has been aged. A few drops of even a modestly priced one (which is what I use most of the time) will do wonders for many foods.

225g / 8oz carrots	*salt and freshly*
225g / 8oz fennel	*ground black pepper*
225g / 8oz courgettes	
125–175g / 4–6oz	
Gruyère or Cheddar	
cheese	

1 Put the kettle on. Scrape the carrots and slice them thinly then put them into a saucepan, pour over boiling water to cover, and simmer for 5 minutes while you prepare the fennel.

2 Trim the fennel, paring away any tough parts on the outer leaves, then slice it into slightly bigger pieces than the carrots. Add to the pan and cook for 5 more minutes.

3 Meanwhile, wash and trim the courgettes, then slice them thinly and add to the pan. Cook for 2–3 minutes, until all the vegetables are tender.

4 Heat the grill. Drain the vegetables (keep the water, if you like; it makes excellent stock). Put the vegetables into a shallow gratin dish and season them lightly with salt and pepper. Then grate or slice the cheese, arrange it on top of the vegetables and put the dish under the grill for 7–10 minutes, until the cheese is golden brown and bubbling.

SERVES 2

GRILLED FENNEL PLATTER

Tender, slightly sweet grilled fennel is combined here with peppery leaves, tangy red peppers and creamy hummus or soft cheese. Serve this platter with some good warm bread.

2 red peppers	*75g / 3oz rocket or*
2 large fennel bulbs	*watercress*
1 tbls olive oil	*125g / 4oz hummus or*
dash of balsamic	*soft cheese, such as*
vinegar	*white goat's cheese,*
salt and freshly	*curd cheese or ricotta*
ground black pepper	

1 Heat the grill. Cut the peppers into quarters, place them cut-side down on a grill pan and grill on high for 10–15 minutes, until the skins have blistered and charred in places. Remove from the grill and cover with a damp cloth.

2 Meanwhile, bring 2.5 cm/1 inch of water to the boil in a saucepan. Trim the fennel, paring away any tough parts on the outer leaves and cutting off the feathery top, then cut it into either six or eight pieces that still hold together at the base. Add to the boiling water, cook for about 8 minutes, until almost completely tender, then drain (keep the water, if you like; it makes excellent stock).

3 Toss the fennel in the oil so that the pieces are completely coated, then spread them out on a grill pan and grill under a high heat for 5–10 minutes or until they are lightly browned, turning them halfway through.

4 Meanwhile, skin and de-seed the red peppers and cut them into strips.

5 Season the fennel and peppers with the balsamic vinegar and salt and pepper to taste. Mix them together if you like, and arrange them on a platter with the rocket or watercress and the hummus or soft cheese.

SERVES 2

BUTTERNUT SQUASH AND GOAT'S CHEESE GRATIN

This unusual gratin is excellent served with a chicory and walnut salad.

1 butternut squash, about 1.1kg / 2½ lb
15g / ½oz butter
1 onion, peeled and chopped
1 garlic clove, crushed
salt and freshly ground black pepper
200g / 7oz goat's cheese log

1. Put the kettle on. Peel and de-seed the butternut squash, then cut the flesh into slices about 6 mm/¼ inch thick. Put them into a saucepan and cover with boiling water, then simmer for about 7 minutes, until tender.
2. Meanwhile, melt the butter in a saucepan, add the onion and garlic, cover and cook gently for about 5 minutes, until the onion is tender.
3. Heat the grill. Drain the butternut squash, reserving the liquid, then return the squash to the pan and add the onion and garlic. You can mash the butternut squash, adding a little of the reserved liquid, if you wish, or leave it as it is. In any case, season with salt and pepper.
4. Put the mixture into a shallow gratin dish. Then slice the cheese thinly, including the rind, and arrange it on top in overlapping slices, like roof tiles. Put it under the grill for 7–10 minutes, until the cheese is golden brown.

SERVES 4

CAULIFLOWER TOMATO CHEESE

This tasty and colourful variation of an old favourite, is good served with a crisp green salad, a quickly cooked green vegetable or something easy such as frozen peas or beans.

1 tbls olive oil
1 onion, peeled and chopped
1 garlic clove, crushed
1 × 400g / 14oz can tomatoes
1 small to medium cauliflower
salt and freshly ground black pepper
125g / 4oz Cheddar or Gruyère cheese, grated

1. First make the tomato sauce: heat the olive oil in a medium pan then fry the onion in it for 5 minutes, until beginning to soften. Add the garlic and tomatoes, breaking the tomatoes up roughly with a wooden spoon.
2. Bring to the boil and let the mixture simmer away for 10–15 minutes, until it is very thick and any excess liquid has evaporated.
3. Meanwhile, wash and trim the cauliflower, breaking it up into even-sized florets. Cook it in 5 cm/2 inches of boiling water for about 5 minutes, until tender, then drain.
4. Heat the grill. Mix the cauliflower florets with the tomato sauce and season well with salt and pepper. Spoon it into a shallow gratin dish, sprinkle with the grated cheese and grill until the cheese is golden brown.

SERVES 2–3

Various types of cheese can be used for this: try blue cheese or feta for a tangy flavour, or one of the flavoured cheeses, such as sage Derby or Cotswold with chives and onion.

MUSHROOMS STUFFED WITH FETA AND RED ONION

These are good served on a base of shredded crisp lettuce, though you could serve them on rounds of toast or fried bread, if you prefer.

1 red onion
olive oil

6 large flat mushrooms
125g / 4oz feta cheese

1 Peel the onion then slice it into thin rings. Heat 1 tablespoon of oil in a pan, add the onion, cover and cook gently for 5–10 minutes, until tender.

2 Heat the grill to high. Wipe the mushrooms and remove the stalks. Brush the caps lightly with olive oil, then place them on a grill pan and grill for 5–10 minutes, until tender and lightly browned. To check if they are done, turn them over and look underneath – it should be moist and tender.

3 Cut the feta cheese into 6 mm/¼ inch cubes. Mix these with the onion in the pan (off the heat).

4 Turn all the mushrooms so that the gills are uppermost, then divide the cheese mixture between them. Put them back under the grill for 5–10 minutes, until the cheese has melted and browned and the mushrooms are piping hot. Serve at once.
SERVES 2

GRILLED MEDITERRANEAN VEGETABLES WITH MOZZARELLA

1 large aubergine,
  about 350g / 12oz
350g / 12oz courgettes
2 tbls olive oil
salt and freshly
  ground black pepper

350g / 12oz tomatoes,
  preferably cherry
  tomatoes
225g / 8oz Mozzarella
  cheese
sprigs of basil

This only needs some good bread – perhaps a crusty Italian-style loaf – to accompany it.

1 Set the grill to high. Cut the aubergine into pieces about 6 mm/¼ inch thick, 5 cm/2 inches long and 2.5 cm/1 inch wide; slice the courgettes into 6 mm/¼ inch rounds. Put them on a grill pan then sprinkle with the olive oil and some salt and

pepper and, using your hands, mix the vegetables so that they all get coated with oil.

2 Put the vegetables under the grill for about 10 minutes, turning them as necessary. Then add the tomatoes – cherry tomatoes whole, others quartered – and grill for a further 5 minutes.

3 Meanwhile, cut the Mozzarella cheese into smallish chunks and add these to the vegetables. Grill for about 5 minutes longer, until the cheese has melted and browned lightly, then tear the basil over the top and serve at once.
SERVES 2

PARSNIP AND HAZELNUT GRATIN

This goes well with some peppery watercress for a quick light lunch or evening meal.

700g / 1½ lb parsnips
15g / ½ oz butter
150ml / 5fl oz soured
  cream

salt and freshly
  ground black pepper
100g / 3½ oz hazelnuts

1 Put the kettle on. Peel the parsnips and cut them into even-sized pieces. Put them in a saucepan, pour over boiling water to cover and simmer for about 10 minutes, until tender.

2 Heat the grill. Drain the parsnips, add the butter and mash well, then stir in the soured cream and season with salt and pepper to taste.

3 Spoon the mixture into a shallow gratin dish. Crush the hazelnuts with a rolling pin or whizz them briefly in a food processor. Scatter them on top of the parsnip mixture.

4 Put the dish under the grill for 5 minutes or so, until the hazelnuts are golden brown.
SERVES 2

OPPOSITE: *Grilled Mediterranean Vegetables with Mozzarella*

POTATO WEDGES
*

Jacket potatoes are a wonderful convenience food because they are so quick to prepare, but the drawback is the long cooking time. Here is a version that is both fast to prepare and fast to cook. This is achieved by cutting and parboiling the potatoes first, then brushing them with olive oil and grilling them to cook them through. They're best served with moist toppings and dips, and a simple crisp salad such as little gem lettuce or chicory and watercress.

BASIC RECIPE

I generally buy a bag of potatoes which are good all-rounders (such as Desiree, King Edward or Maris Piper) and use the larger ones for this recipe; the large ones which supermarkets label 'baking potatoes' often cost much more than the ones you pick out yourself!

2 × 225–350g / 8–12oz potatoes   olive oil
                         sea salt

1. Put the kettle on. Scrub the potatoes, cut each one in half lengthways and then in half again, to make four long wedges.
2. Put the potato wedges into a saucepan, cover with boiling water and bring back to the boil. Cook for 5 minutes from the time the water boils, then drain thoroughly.
3. Meanwhile, heat the grill. Brush the drained potato wedges all over with olive oil, then put them on a baking sheet or a grill pan and place them under the grill.
4. Grill on high for 10–15 minutes, until the potatoes are tender right through and golden brown, turning them as necessary. Remove from the grill, sprinkle with sea salt, then serve with any of the toppings below.
SERVES 2

VARIATIONS

1 POTATO WEDGES WITH HERBS

Sprinkle the potatoes with fresh rosemary or thyme before grilling; caraway seeds are good, too, if you like the flavour.

2 POTATO STEAKS

These are made in the same way, except that this time you cut the potatoes into slices about 1 cm / ½ inch thick – like steaks – instead of into wedges.

TOPPINGS

All these toppings make enough for two large potatoes. As well as the recipes below, you could try the following suggestions: soured cream mixed with horseradish sauce or chopped fresh chives; guacamole (see page 21); good-quality bought pesto or homemade (see page 59); soft goat's cheese, cream cheese or cottage cheese; hummus; garlic butter; or, of course, plenty of butter and grated cheese.

— 1 —
MUSHROOMS IN SOURED CREAM

225g / 8oz chestnut mushrooms   salt and freshly ground black pepper
25g / 1oz butter   chopped fresh chives
1 garlic clove, crushed
150ml / 5fl oz soured cream

1. Wipe and slice the mushrooms. Melt the butter in a saucepan and add the mushrooms then cook, uncovered, for about 5 minutes, until tender.
2. Add the garlic and cook for a further 1–2 minutes, then remove from the heat.
3. Just before you are ready to serve, put the pan back on the heat and get the mushrooms sizzling again. Then add the soured cream and stir until it has heated through; don't let it boil or it will curdle. Remove from the heat, season, and serve with some chopped chives on top.

— 2 —
RED AND YELLOW PEPPER SALSA

Start making this before you prepare the potato wedges, so the peppers can be grilling while you scrub and boil the potatoes.

1 red pepper	**salt and freshly**
1 yellow pepper	**ground black pepper**
2 large tomatoes	

☐1 Heat the grill. Cut the peppers in half and put them cut-side down on a grill pan, then grill them under a fierce heat until they are blistered and charred in places. Remove them from the grill and cover with a damp tea towel.

☐2 Pour boiling water over the tomatoes, leave for a few seconds until the skins loosen, then drain them and cover with cold water. Remove the skins with a sharp knife. Chop the tomatoes and put them into a bowl.

☐3 Remove the skin from the pepper halves – it will peel off easily – and also remove any seeds. Thinly slice the peppers and add to the tomatoes. Mix well and season with salt and pepper.

— 3 —
CHILLI-TOMATO SAUCE

1 tbls olive oil	**chilli powder**
1 onion, peeled and	**salt, freshly ground**
chopped	**black pepper and**
1 garlic clove, crushed	**sugar**
1 × 400g / 14oz can	
tomatoes	

☐1 Heat the oil in a saucepan, then put in the onion, cover and cook for 10 minutes.

☐2 Stir in the garlic and cook for 1–2 minutes, then pour in the tomatoes, breaking them up with the spoon. Add a pinch or so of chilli powder to taste. Cook for 10–15 minutes, uncovered, until the mixture is thick.

☐3 Season with salt and pepper then add extra chilli powder if the sauce needs more of a kick, and a dash of sugar if necessary.

— 4 —
HERB CREAM CHEESE

Put a packet of garlic and herb cream cheese into a bowl and add 2 tablespoons of hot water, then beat it until it is smooth and creamy, adding more water if necessary to achieve this consistency.

— 5 —
ROMESCO SAUCE

1 red pepper	**piece of dried red chilli**
olive oil	**or a pinch of chilli**
25g / 1oz white bread	**powder**
25g / 1oz flaked	**1 tomato, skinned and**
almonds	**quartered**
1 small garlic clove,	**salt and freshly**
peeled	**ground black pepper**
	balsamic vinegar

☐1 Heat the grill. Cut the pepper in half, put the halves cut-side down on a grill pan and grill under a fierce heat for about 10 minutes, until they are blistered and charred in places. Remove from the grill and cover with a damp tea towel.

☐2 Meanwhile, heat a little olive oil in a frying pan and fry the bread until it is crisp and golden brown on both sides. Then remove it from the pan and put in the almonds, frying them until they are golden brown.

☐3 When the pepper is cool enough to handle, peel off the skin, remove the seeds and stem, and cut the pepper into rough chunks. Put it into a food processor with the bread, roughly torn, and the almonds, garlic, chilli and tomato. Whizz to a creamy purée.

☐4 Season with salt and coarsely ground black pepper then mix in a few drops of balsamic vinegar to taste.

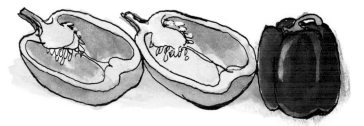

— 6 —
CREAMY SWEETCORN

25g / 1oz butter
2 tbls plain flour
300ml / ½ pint milk
½–1 red pepper,
  chopped (optional)

225g / 8oz frozen
  sweetcorn
salt and freshly
  ground black pepper

1 Melt the butter in a saucepan, then stir in the flour. Let it cook for a minute or two, then stir in the milk. Bring it to the boil, stirring, to make a smooth sauce. If you are using the red pepper, add this now, then leave the sauce to simmer over a low heat for 5 minutes.
2 Add the frozen sweetcorn and cook for a further 3–4 minutes, then season to taste with salt and pepper.

— 7 —
CHEDDAR CHEESE AND SPRING ONION DIP

15g / ½oz soft butter
125g / 4oz Cheddar
  cheese, grated
4 tbls single cream or
  milk

2 spring onions
salt and freshly
  ground black pepper

1 Put the butter into a bowl and add the cheese and cream or milk. Beat to make a creamy mixture.
2 Trim and chop the spring onions then stir them into the dip and season to taste.

— 8 —
GREEN HERB MAYONNAISE

Put 4 tablespoons of good-quality mayonnaise, or 2 tablespoons of mayonnaise and 2 tablespoons of yogurt, into a small bowl and stir in 4 tablespoons of finely chopped fresh herbs, such as parsley, chives, tarragon, chervil.

— 9 —
VERY MINTY TZATZIKI

½ cucumber
salt and freshly
  ground black pepper
150ml / 5fl oz thick
  Greek yogurt

½ garlic clove, crushed
4 tbls chopped fresh
  mint

1 Peel the cucumber and cut it into small dice. Put these into a sieve, sprinkle with salt, cover with a plate and a weight and leave on one side to draw out excess moisture.
2 Put the yogurt into a bowl and mix in the garlic and most of the fresh mint.
3 Just before you are ready to serve, pat the cucumber dry on kitchen paper then stir it into the yogurt mixture. Check the seasoning, then sprinkle the rest of the mint on top.

— 10 —
COLESLAW

Home-made coleslaw is so much nicer than the bought variety and it's dead simple to make.

125g / 4oz cabbage
2 small carrots
8 tbls good-quality
  mayonnaise, or a
  mixture of
  mayonnaise and
  plain yogurt

2 spring onions
  (optional)
salt and freshly
  ground black pepper

1 Wash the cabbage, then shred it finely and put it into a bowl.
2 Scrub or scrape the carrots then grate them into the bowl.
3 Stir in the mayonnaise or mayonnaise and yogurt. Trim and chop the spring onions, if you're using them, and add them to the bowl, too. Season with salt and pepper to taste.

OPPOSITE: **Baked Potato Wedges and Steaks topped with Pesto, Romesco Sauce and herbs**

SPICED VEGETABLE DISHES
✳

SPICED MIXED VEGETABLES IN CREAMY SAUCE

This is a very simple spiced vegetable dish and I think it's nicest served with some plain basmati rice. You can use all kinds of different vegetables, and if you don't like the idea of the soured cream (which has the same fat content as single cream) you could substitute single cream or even milk.

There's no need to peel fresh ginger if you're grating it: just use a fairly fine grater.

175g / 6oz carrots
175g / 6oz potatoes
175g / 6oz courgettes
125g / 4oz frozen peas
2 tbls oil
knob of fresh ginger
   root
2 tbls ground
   coriander
½ tsp garam masala
150ml / 5fl oz soured
   cream
salt and freshly
   ground black pepper
chopped fresh
   coriander

1. Put the kettle on. Scrape the carrots and slice them thinly; peel the potatoes and cut them into bigger pieces. Put them into a saucepan, pour over boiling water to cover, then simmer for about 10 minutes, until they are nearly tender.
2. Meanwhile, wash, trim and slice the courgettes. Add them to the pan, along with the frozen peas, and cook for 2–3 minutes, until just tender. Drain the vegetables (keep the water, if you like; it makes excellent stock).
3. Heat the oil in a large saucepan, grate the ginger and add it to the pan. Cook for a few seconds, then stir in the ground coriander and garam masala and cook for a few seconds more.
4. Add the cooked vegetables and stir over the heat until they are coated with the spices, then stir in the soured cream and continue to cook for a few minutes more until the cream is heated through. Season with salt and pepper and serve sprinkled with chopped coriander.

SERVES 2

MIXED VEGETABLE CURRY

This makes quite a large quantity and tastes very good the next day, reheated.

1 onion
1 large carrot
2 tbls olive oil
1 potato, about
   225g / 8oz
knob of fresh ginger
   root
1 garlic clove
1 green chilli
½ tsp turmeric powder
2 tbls ground
   coriander
6 curry leaves or ¼ tsp
   curry powder
salt and freshly
   ground black pepper
½ medium cauliflower
125g / 4oz green beans
fresh coriander, if
   available

1. Peel and chop the onion; scrape and thinly slice the carrot. Heat the oil in a large saucepan, put in the onion and carrot, then cover and cook gently. Peel the potato, cut it into even-sized pieces and add these to the pan.
2. Grate the ginger and crush the garlic; halve, deseed and chop the chilli. Add these to the pan along with the turmeric, ground coriander and curry leaves or powder and stir well for 1–2 minutes so that everything gets coated with the spices.
3. Add 450ml/¾ pint of water, 2 teaspoons of salt and a grinding of pepper to the pan. Bring to the boil, then leave to simmer, covered, for 5 minutes.
4. Meanwhile, wash the cauliflower and remove the leaves, saving any that are tender; chop these up. Break the cauliflower into florets of roughly equal size. Wash and trim the green beans.
5. Stir the cauliflower and beans into the pan then cover and cook for 7–10 minutes or until all the vegetables are just tender. If the mixture looks too liquid, turn up the heat and let it bubble away for a minute or two. Then check the seasoning and serve. It's nice with some fresh coriander snipped over the top, if you have some.

SERVES 2–4

SPICED SPINACH AND POTATOES

I love the combination of potatoes and dark green leafy vegetables. It's found in a number of peasant dishes around the world. From Ireland there's the soothing Colcannon (see page 100), while India offers this spicy mixture, very different in character yet equally appealing. It's good with some dal (see page 81), if you've time to make that too, otherwise just serve with plain rice or Indian breads.

225g / 8oz potatoes
2 tbls oil
1 red chilli, fresh or
    dried
2 tsp cumin seeds
½ tsp turmeric
1 onion, peeled and
    chopped
1 garlic clove, crushed
450g / 1lb tender fresh
    or frozen leaf spinach
salt and freshly
    ground black pepper

1. Peel the potatoes and cut them into 1 cm/ ½ inch cubes. Heat the oil in a large saucepan, then put in the whole chilli, the cumin seeds and turmeric; stir over the heat for a few seconds, letting the spices fry but not burn.

2. Add the potatoes, onion and garlic then cover and leave them to cook gently for about 15 minutes, or until the potatoes are tender. Stir from time to time and add 1–2 tablespoons of water if the vegetables start to stick.

3. Meanwhile, cook the spinach: if you are using fresh spinach, wash it and put the leaves, still damp, into a large saucepan without any extra water. Cover and cook for 5–8 minutes until tender. If you are using frozen spinach, cook it in 6 mm/¼ inch of boiling water for about 3 minutes. Drain the spinach well.

4. Add the spinach to the potato mixture and remove the chilli. Season with salt and pepper and then serve.

SERVES 2

THAI-FLAVOURED AUBERGINE IN COCONUT MILK

Aubergine cooked like this is rich and full of flavour. I like it best served with some plain boiled busmati rice. The aubergine won't spoil if it's cooked ahead of time and reheated – in fact this gives the flavours a chance to develop. Don't leave out the fresh coriander; it really is essential for this dish.

1 tbls dark sesame oil
1 onion, peeled and
    chopped
1 garlic clove, crushed
1 green or red chilli
1 large aubergine
1 tbls coconut milk
    powder
salt, freshly ground
    black pepper, and
    sugar
1 packet of fresh
    coriander

1. Heat the oil in a medium saucepan, add the onion and garlic, then cover and cook gently for 5 minutes, until softened.

2. Meanwhile, halve, de-seed and chop the chilli; wash the aubergine and remove the stem. Cut the aubergine into chunky pieces roughly 1 cm/½ inch square. Add the chilli and aubergine to the pan, then cover and cook for a further 5 minutes. There won't be enough oil for the aubergine to soak up, but that's all right.

3. Put the coconut milk powder into a jug and stir in 300ml/½ pint of water, then pour this into the pan and bring to the boil. Cover and leave to simmer for about 20 minutes, or until the aubergine is tender and the liquid has reduced to a shiny sauce. If there is too much liquid at this stage, just turn up the heat and let it boil, uncovered, for a few more minutes.

4. Season with plenty of salt and freshly ground black pepper, and some sugar – I find it needs about half a teaspoonful for the right balance of flavours. Then snip in a generous amount of fresh coriander. You can serve the aubergine straight away, if you like, but it is also extremely good eaten at room temperature.

SERVES 2

You can buy coconut milk powder at Chinese shops and some large supermarkets. If you can't get it you can substitute canned coconut milk, or use desiccated coconut as described on page 85.

FRITTERS & FRIED VEGETABLES

Although most health-conscious people are cutting down on their fat intake, fritters can still have their place in a healthy diet as a delicious occasional treat – and they're quick and easy to make. Serve them with low-fat accompaniments such as salad, steamed vegetables or plain rice.

ONION BHAJEES

A wok is excellent for deep-frying because it has a large surface area but does not require a great deal of oil. Groundnut and corn are two of the most suitable oils for deep-frying; but try not to re-use the oil too many times.

These are often served as a nibble, but they make a filling meal served with some plainly cooked rice, chutney and perhaps a raita.

125g / 4oz chick pea
  (gram) flour
2 tsp ground coriander
1 tsp ground cumin
pinch of cayenne
  pepper

1 tsp salt
oil for deep-frying
1 onion, peeled and
  finely chopped
1 tbls chopped fresh
  coriander (optional)

☐1 Sift the chick pea flour into a bowl with the ground coriander, cumin and cayenne. Add the salt, then pour in 150ml/5fl oz of tepid water and stir to make a batter.

☐2 Heat some oil in a deep-fryer or large saucepan. Stir the chopped onion, and the fresh coriander if you are using this, into the batter, then, when the oil is hot, drop teaspoonfuls of the mixture into the pan and fry, in batches, for about 5 minutes, until they are really crisp and the onion is cooked through.

☐3 Drain the bhajees on kitchen paper and keep the first batch warm, uncovered, while you cook the rest. Then serve immediately.
SERVES 2

VEGETABLES IN CHICK PEA BATTER

This is more of a snack than a main meal. Serve with mango chutney and a raita made by stirring fresh coriander, mint or crushed garlic into plain yogurt.

75g / 3oz chick pea
  (gram) flour
½ tsp cumin seeds
½ tsp ground coriander
good pinch of cayenne
  pepper
½ tsp salt

1 tsp oil
oil for deep-frying
175–225g / 6–8oz
  mixed vegetables:
  onions, cauliflower
  and courgettes

☐1 Make the batter: sift the chick pea flour into a bowl then stir in the spices and salt. Add the oil and about 125–150ml/4–5fl oz warm water to make a fairly thick batter.

☐2 Heat some oil in a deep-fryer, wok or large saucepan. Meanwhile, prepare the vegetables. They need to be in fairly small pieces so that they will have cooked by the time the batter is crisp. Peel onions and slice them into rings; cut cauliflower into fairly small florets and courgettes into batons or rounds.

☐3 Dip the vegetables in the batter and shake off the excess. Fry them in the oil, in batches, for a few minutes, until they are crisp and golden brown on the outside, tender within. Drain on kitchen paper and serve at once, before they lose their crispness.
SERVES 2

OPPOSITE: *Vegetables in Chick Pea Batter*

MUSHROOMS IN BATTER WITH GARLIC MAYONNAISE

The batter for these is taken from Elizabeth David's French Provincial Cooking, *except that I don't usually let it stand for two hours and certainly not if I'm in a hurry. As Elizabeth David says, it always comes out light and crisp. The mushrooms make a good main course if you serve them with watercress or some other salad.*

125g / 4oz plain flour
3 tbls olive oil
salt and freshly
  ground black pepper
oil for deep-frying
225g / 8oz baby button
  mushrooms, really
  tiny ones are best

1 garlic clove, crushed
4 tbls good bought
  mayonnaise, or
  a mixture of
  mayonnaise and
  yogurt
1 egg white

1   Sift the flour into a bowl, then add the olive oil, 1 teaspoon of salt, a grinding of pepper and 150ml/5fl oz of tepid water. Beat well until it becomes a smooth cream.

2   Heat some oil in a deep-fryer or a large saucepan. Wipe the mushrooms with damp kitchen paper, then put them on a plate and sprinkle them with salt and a grinding of pepper. Mix the garlic with the mayonnaise or mayonnaise and yogurt.

3   Whisk the egg white until it is stiff then fold it gently into the batter. When the oil is hot, dip the mushrooms into the batter to coat them, then drop them, a few at a time, into the hot oil. Let them fry for about 3–4 minutes, until golden brown and crisp. It's important that they are in the oil long enough to cook through.

4   Drain the mushrooms on kitchen paper and keep the first lot warm, uncovered, while you cook the rest. Then serve immediately, while they're still really crisp, with the garlic mayonnaise.

SERVES 2–3

Test the temperature of oil for deep-frying by dipping a wooden chopstick or the handle of a wooden spoon into it: if the oil is hot enough it should immediately form bubbles around it.

CHILLI AND ONION CORN CAKES

These crisp golden-brown savoury cakes make an excellent main course served with a lettuce or tomato salad and some cooked rice. They are also good with chutney, or a sauce made by stirring chopped fresh herbs into plain yogurt.

1 × 350g / 12oz can
  sweetcorn, drained
125g / 4oz instant
  polenta
2 eggs
50g / 2oz fresh
  Parmesan cheese,
  grated
4 tbls milk

4 spring onions
1 green chilli
salt and freshly
  ground black pepper
oil for shallow-frying
a little extra grated
  Parmesan to serve
  (optional)

1   Put the sweetcorn into a bowl with the polenta. Add the eggs, grated Parmesan and milk, and mix together well.

2   Trim and finely chop the spring onions; halve, de-seed and finely chop the chilli, washing your hands well afterwards. Add the spring onions and chilli to the sweetcorn mixture and season with salt and pepper.

3   Pour enough oil into a frying pan to cover the base thinly. When it is hot, drop heaped table-spoonfuls of the mixture into the pan to make flat 'cakes'. Fry them for about 2 minutes, until crisp and brown underneath, then flip them over and fry the other side for the same amount of time.

4   Drain the cakes on kitchen paper and keep them warm while you fry the remaining mixture. Serve immediately, sprinkled with some more grated Parmesan, if you like.

SERVES 4

QUICK POTATO PANCAKES

2 large potatoes, about   *butter*
  450g / 1lb altogether   *oil*
1 tsp salt

1. Peel the potatoes, then grate them on the coarse side of a grater. Mix the grated potatoes with the salt (don't rinse the potatoes; the starch is necessary to hold the pancakes together).

2. Heat a knob of butter and 1 tablespoon of oil in a frying pan and put in spoonfuls of the potato mixture, flattening them with the back of the spoon. After about 3 minutes, when the underneath is crisp and brown, turn the pancakes over and cook the other side for about 3 minutes, until brown.

3. Drain on kitchen paper, then cook the remaining mixture in the same way, adding more butter and oil if necessary. Serve immediately.

SERVES 2

POTATO KOFTAS WITH SPICY BEAN SAUCE

This consists of crisp potato balls served with a spiced bean mixture. It was inspired by a recipe in The Flavours of Gujerati, *published by Virani Food Products, from which I've adapted the koftas.*

450g / 1lb potatoes
1 tbls olive oil
1 onion, peeled and
  chopped
1 garlic clove, crushed
1 × 400g / 14oz can
  tomatoes
oil for deep-frying
2 tbls lemon juice
3 tbls cornflour
chilli powder

1 tbls chopped fresh
  coriander
salt, freshly ground
  black pepper, and
  sugar
50g / 2oz dried
  breadcrumbs
1 × 425g / 15oz can red
  kidney beans,
  drained
1 × 350g / 12oz can
  sweetcorn, drained

1. Half-fill a medium-sized pan with water and bring to the boil for the potatoes. Peel the potatoes and cut them into 1 cm/½ inch cubes. Add them to the water and cook for about 10 minutes, until tender. Drain and mash the potatoes.

2. Start making the sauce: heat the olive oil in a medium pan then fry the onion in it for 5 minutes, until beginning to soften. Stir in the garlic and tomatoes, breaking the tomatoes up roughly with the spoon. Bring to the boil and simmer for 10–15 minutes, until the sauce is very thick with no excess liquid.

3. Start heating some oil for deep-frying, but keep your eye on it. Then finish making the potato koftas: add the lemon juice, cornflour, a pinch of chilli powder, and the chopped coriander to the potatoes, then season with some salt, pepper and perhaps a pinch of sugar, if necessary.

4. Form the potato mixture into balls about the size of walnuts and roll them in the dried breadcrumbs to coat them lightly.

5. When the oil is hot enough, put in a batch of the koftas and fry for 3–4 minutes, until crisp and golden brown. Drain them on kitchen paper and keep them warm while you fry the rest.

6. Meanwhile, add the kidney beans and sweetcorn to the tomato sauce, then season with salt, pepper, chilli powder to taste, and a pinch of sugar, if necessary. Warm over a gentle heat until the beans and sweetcorn are heated through. Spoon the bean mixture on to warmed plates, top with the koftas and serve at once.

SERVES 4

The simplest of potato pancakes, quickly made and delicious. Try serving them with soured cream, or apple or cranberry sauce, plus a salad or green vegetable. They are also surprisingly good with hummus.

ROSTI WITH SPRING ONIONS

Rösti is very quick and simple to prepare and makes a wonderful snack. This version includes spring onions but you can vary it by adding different ingredients such as herbs, onion, grated fresh ginger and spices. It's good served with a juicy salad such as tomato and basil, and perhaps some yogurt with fresh herbs stirred into it. Alternatively, serve the crisp rösti with mushrooms in soured cream (see page 106).

450g / 1lb potatoes	**salt**
small bunch of spring onions	**4 tbls oil**

1. Scrub the potatoes then put them into a saucepan, cover with cold water and bring to the boil. Boil them for about 5 minutes, until they are just beginning to get tender on the outside. Meanwhile, trim and chop the spring onions then cut them into long, thin pieces.

2. Drain the potatoes and leave them until they are cool enough to handle, then slip off the skins using a small sharp knife and your fingers. Grate the potatoes coarsely and season with a little salt, then mix in the spring onions.

3. Heat the oil in a frying pan, then add the potato mixture and press it down with a spatula to make one large round. Fry over a moderate heat for about 7 minutes, until crisp and brown underneath. Turn the rösti over by turning it out on to a plate then sliding it back into the frying pan.

4. Continue to cook the rösti until the second side is browned and crisp, then drain on kitchen paper, sprinkle with salt and serve at once, cut into wedges.

SERVES 2

OPPOSITE: *(left) Rösti with Spring Onions, (right) Crisp Fried Aubergine with Parsley Sauce*

CRISP FRIED AUBERGINE WITH PARSLEY SAUCE

I love these crisp slices of aubergine with their creamy sauce. You can serve them just as they are or make more of a meal of them by adding a cooked green vegetable or salad – and even some chips if you've got time to do them!

1 medium aubergine, about 225g / 8oz	**FOR THE PARSLEY SAUCE**
50g / 2oz ground almonds	**25g / 1oz butter**
1 tsp chopped fresh dill	**20g / ¾ oz plain flour**
1 egg, beaten	**300 ml / ½ pint milk**
light olive oil for frying	**4 tbls cream (optional)**
fresh dill to garnish	**2–3 tbls chopped fresh parsley**
	salt and freshly ground black pepper

1. First make the parsley sauce: melt the butter in a saucepan and stir in the flour; when it froths, stir in half the milk, then beat well until it thickens. Stir in the rest of the milk and keep stirring vigorously over the heat, until the sauce is thick and smooth.

2. Let the sauce simmer over a very low heat for about 7 minutes, checking to make sure it doesn't stick or burn. Then stir in the cream, if you're using this, the parsley and plenty of salt and pepper.

3. Wash the aubergine and remove the stem. Cut the aubergine lengthwise into slices about 6 mm / ¼ inch thick then season with salt and pepper.

4. Mix the ground almonds with the dill and some salt and pepper and put them on a flat plate. Dip the aubergine slices first in beaten egg and then into the ground almond mixture, making sure they are well-coated with almonds on both sides.

5. Heat a little oil in a large frying pan then put in the aubergine slices. You'll probably have to cook them in two batches; turn on the grill so that you can keep the first batch warm. Fry the aubergine over a moderate heat for about 4 minutes per side, until crisp and golden on both sides and tender inside when pierced with a knife. Drain on kitchen paper, garnish with dill and serve with the sauce.

SERVES 2

STIR-FRIES

—— ✳ ——

THAI STIR-FRY

This stir-fry is delicately flavoured with coconut milk but has the added kick of hot red chilli and the tang of lemon grass and fresh coriander. It's delicious with some plain boiled rice; put this on to cook first of all.

If you can't find fresh lemon grass, substitute the grated rind of half a lemon.

40g / 1½ oz creamed coconut	2 tbls groundnut oil
1 dried red chilli	50g / 2oz raw peanuts
1 large carrot	1 lemon grass stalk
125g / 4oz mangetout	1 garlic clove, crushed
125g / 4oz baby sweetcorn	25g / 1oz fresh coriander leaves, roughly chopped
1 bunch of spring onions	salt and freshly ground black pepper
1 red pepper	

1 First prepare the coconut milk: either grate the coconut or cut it into thin flakes, then put it into a small saucepan with 150ml/5fl oz of water and bring to the boil. Stir until the coconut has melted, then remove from the heat and leave on one side.

2 Halve the chilli and scrape away and discard the seeds if you prefer less heat. Then chop the chilli finely and add it to the coconut cream.

3 Scrape the carrot and slice it thinly; top and tail the mangetout; halve the baby sweetcorn if they are large; trim and chop the spring onions; halve, de-seed and slice the red pepper.

4 Heat the oil in a wok or very large saucepan. When it is smoking, put in the peanuts and fry them for a few minutes until they smell and look roasted, then add all the vegetables and stir-fry for 1–2 minutes.

5 Finely chop the lemon grass and add it with the garlic to the vegetables; continue to stir-fry for 1–2 minutes until the vegetables are hot but still quite crisp, then pour in the coconut cream and stir-fry for a few seconds until this is hot. Add the coriander, season with salt and pepper and serve.
SERVES 2

CHINESE VEGETABLE STIR-FRY

The vegetables suggested here provide a good mixture of colours and textures but you can use different ones if you prefer. Some plain basmati rice goes well with this – put it on to cook before you start preparing the stir-fry.

To cook plain basmati rice, allow 50g/2oz rice and 300ml/½ pint of water per person. Wash the rice in a sieve under the cold tap, then bring the water to the boil, pour in the rice and boil fast for about 10 minutes, or until it is tender but still firm. Drain in a sieve and rinse with hot water, then put it back in the pan and keep warm until needed.

1 red onion	knob of fresh ginger root, grated
2 carrots	1 tbls cornflour
½ head of Chinese leaves	2 tbls good-quality soy sauce, such as Kikkoman
125g / 4oz broccoli	1 tsp sugar
125g / 4oz baby sweetcorn	good pinch of Chinese five-spice powder
125g / 4oz button mushrooms	salt and freshly ground black pepper
1 tbls groundnut oil	
1 garlic clove, crushed	

1 Peel, halve and slice the onion; scrape the carrots and cut them diagonally into fairly thin slices; wash the Chinese leaves and cut them into fairly chunky slices; separate the broccoli into small florets, removing any tough stem; halve the baby sweetcorn if they are large; wash and slice the mushrooms.

2 Heat the oil in a wok or very large saucepan. When it is smoking, put in all the vegetables and the garlic and ginger and stir-fry for 2–3 minutes, until they are wilting but still crunchy.

3 Put the cornflour into a small bowl or cup and mix with the soy sauce and sugar. Add this to the pan and stir-fry for 1–2 minutes longer, until the mixture has thickened and clings to the vegetables.

4 Add the five-spice powder and some salt and pepper and serve at once.
SERVES 2

OPPOSITE: *Thai Stir-fry*

MANGETOUT AND MUSHROOM STIR-FRY

This is good served simply with some rice, and it also goes extremely well with the red pepper and cashew nut stir-fry, if you want to serve two different dishes for four people.

2 tbls oil
1 large onion, peeled
  and chopped
knob of fresh ginger
  root
1 garlic clove, crushed
225g / 8oz mangetout
225g / 8oz button
  mushrooms

1 tbls cornflour
1 tsp sugar
1 tbls sherry
1 tbls soy sauce
salt and freshly
  ground black pepper

1 Heat the oil in a large frying pan or wok, put in the onion then cover and cook gently. Grate the ginger and add it to the pan, along with the garlic.

2 Wash and trim the mangetout and mushrooms as necessary, slicing or halving the mushrooms if they are large.

3 In a cup or small bowl, mix together the cornflour, sugar, sherry and soy sauce. Leave this on one side for the moment.

4 When the onion is almost done, add the mangetout and mushrooms and stir-fry for 2–3 minutes, until just tender. Then give the soy sauce mixture a quick stir and pour it in; stir until the mixture has thickened and coats the vegetables thinly. Season with salt and pepper, then serve.

SERVES 2

RED PEPPER AND CASHEW NUT STIR-FRY

This is my recreation of a dish I enjoyed in a Chinese restaurant – the combination of soft, sweet peppers and chewy cashews is very good. Serve it with some plain boiled rice.

2 large red peppers
2 tbls oil
1 hot red chilli, fresh
  or dried
100g / 3½oz cashew
  nuts

1 tbls cornflour
1 tbls soy sauce
salt and sugar

1 Halve, de-seed and slice the red peppers. Heat the oil in a wok or large saucepan and put in the whole chilli; let it sizzle away for a few seconds.

2 Add the peppers and cashew nuts to the pan, cover and cook gently for about 5 minutes, stirring occasionally. Add 300 ml / ½ pint of water and cook for a further 10 minutes, until the peppers are very tender.

3 Meanwhile, blend the cornflour to a paste with the soy sauce, adding a little water if necessary. Pour this into the pepper mixture, stirring until it thickens.

4 Taste, and season with salt and a pinch of sugar if necessary, then serve.

SERVES 2

MAIN-COURSE SALADS
✳

WARM JERUSALEM ARTICHOKE SALAD

This is very filling and makes a good meal for the end of winter or very early spring. The hard-boiled eggs add colour, but they can be swapped with Brazil (or other) nuts for a vegan dish.

2 eggs
450g / 1lb Jerusalem
  artichokes
1 tbls olive oil
1 tbls balsamic
  vinegar

salt and freshly
  ground black pepper
a few lettuce leaves
2 tbls chopped fresh
  chives

[1]   Hard-boil the eggs by simmering them in a pan of boiling water for 7–10 minutes. Then drain them, cover with cold water and leave to cool.
[2]   Meanwhile, peel the Jerusalem artichokes, dropping them straight into cold water when they're done to keep them white. Then cut them into 6 mm/¼ inch slices.
[3]   Heat the oil in a medium saucepan and put in the artichoke slices; shake the pan to coat them with the oil, then cover and leave to cook very gently for about 20 minutes, until they are completely tender.
[4]   Meanwhile, shell the eggs, rinse them under cold water and cut them into quarters or sixths.
[5]   Remove the artichokes from the heat, stir in the balsamic vinegar and season with salt and pepper. Arrange the lettuce leaves on a serving plate or two individual plates. Spoon the artichokes on top and sprinkle the chives over them, then arrange the hard-boiled eggs around the edges. Serve at once.
SERVES 2

ITALIAN COUNTRY SALAD

This is a pleasant mixture of flavours and textures. Serve it simply with some country-style bread.

4 eggs
225g / 8oz fine green
  beans
225g / 8oz courgettes
1 garlic clove, crushed
1 tbls red wine vinegar

3 tbls olive oil
salt and freshly
  ground black pepper
125g / 4oz black olives
50–125g / 2–4oz
  Parmesan cheese

[1]   Hard-boil the eggs by simmering them in a pan of boiling water for 7–10 minutes. Then drain them, cover with cold water and leave to cool.
[2]   Meanwhile, bring 2.5 cm/1 inch of water to the boil in a large saucepan. Wash and trim the beans; wash and slice the courgettes. When the water boils, put in the beans and boil for 1–2 minutes, then add the courgettes and cook for a further 1–2 minutes, until just tender. Drain the vegetables.
[3]   Put the garlic into a salad bowl with the vinegar, olive oil and some salt and pepper. Mix well, then add the vegetables (which can still be hot). Stir gently.
[4]   Shell the hard-boiled eggs and rinse them under cold water, then slice them and add them to the bowl, along with the olives.
[5]   Cut the Parmesan cheese into thin flakes with a sharp knife or a swivel-bladed potato peeler and add these to the salad. Toss all the ingredients gently and serve.
SERVES 4

Jerusalem artichokes have such a delicious, almost nutty flavour that it's a pity many people avoid them because of their anti-social effects on the digestive system... I think their reputation in this respect is a bit exaggerated; anyway, they're certainly worth trying, and enjoying on the right occasions.

GREEN BEAN, AVOCADO AND CASHEW NUT SALAD

This is a rich and filling salad which just needs some good bread to go with it.

175g / 6oz thin green
  beans
1 medium avocado
juice of ½ lemon
1 tbls olive oil

50g / 2oz roasted
  cashew nuts
salt and freshly
  ground black pepper

1 Bring 1 cm/½ inch of water to the boil in a large pan for the green beans. Trim the beans then add them to the boiling water, cover and cook for 2–4 minutes or until just tender. Drain, and put them into a bowl.

2 Halve the avocado, remove the stone and skin, then cut it into long, thin slices.

3 Put the avocado slices into the bowl with the beans and add the lemon juice, olive oil, cashew nuts and a seasoning of salt and pepper. Go easy on the salt if the cashew nuts are already salted. Serve the salad at once.

SERVES 2

WALDORF SALAD IN RADICCHIO

This is a light version of the classic Waldorf salad and it includes grapes as well as apples, for a change. It's nicest made with freshly shelled walnuts, if you have time to crack them, and it makes a good lunch or light supper dish, perhaps served with a slice of malt bread or fruit loaf spread with cream cheese or curd cheese.

OPPOSITE: *(top) Green Bean, Avocado and Cashew Nut Salad, (right) Thai Cabbage Salad, (bottom) Waldorf Salad in Radicchio*

1 celery heart
225g / 8oz Cox's apples
125g / 4oz purple or
  red grapes
2 tbls good-quality
  mayonnaise

2 tbls plain yogurt
salt and freshly
  ground black pepper
25g / 1oz walnuts
few leaves of radicchio

1 Wash and slice the celery; peel, core and slice the apples; wash, halve and pip the grapes. Put all these ingredients into a bowl with the mayonnaise, yogurt and some salt and pepper to taste and mix gently until combined.

2 Stir in half the walnuts, then spoon the mixture into the radicchio leaves and sprinkle the remaining nuts on top. Serve at once.

SERVES 2

THAI CABBAGE SALAD

1 hot red chilli
1 lemon grass stalk
225g / 8oz white
  cabbage
125g / 4oz baby
  sweetcorn
25g / 1oz fresh
  coriander

1 tbls sesame oil
1 tbls soy sauce
juice of ½ lime
salt and freshly
  ground black pepper
sugar (optional)

1 Finely chop the chilli, scraping out and discarding the seeds if you prefer. Finely slice the lemon grass, removing any tough stem, then finely shred the cabbage, slice the baby sweetcorn into rounds and chop the coriander.

2 Heat the oil in a pan and put in the chilli and lemon grass; fry for a few seconds, then add the cabbage and baby sweetcorn; stir-fry for 1–2 minutes, until wilted, then remove from the heat, and add the soy sauce and lime juice. Mix well, then lightly stir in the coriander leaves. Season with salt, pepper and perhaps a pinch of sugar. Serve the salad while still warm.

SERVES 2–4

The Thai flavourings in this salad make it quite unusual. Serve it as a side salad with a main dish or with something simple – and most unoriental! – such as grilled cheese on toast.

FRUIT

If you're looking for something to give you a quick burst of energy, fruit beats sugary convenience foods any day: it's easy to carry, sweet and delicious to eat, and doesn't make you fat or rot your teeth. But fruit isn't just for snacking. It can also be the basis of starters, such as Three-Pear Salad, and light main courses, such as Apricots with Ricotta and Mint or Tarragon Pear with Cream Cheese. And, of course, fruit is perfect for quick nutritious desserts, from light, refreshing Peaches in Wine or Rhubarb and Ginger Compote to more substantial puddings such as Blueberry Crumble.

FRUIT SALADS & SAVOURY FRUIT DISHES
✳

MELON WITH STRAWBERRIES AND MINT

Although most often served as a starter, melon makes a pleasant dessert or even a light, refreshing snack. Small round melons with green flesh, such as baby Ogen or Galia, are ideal for this, if you can get them; otherwise use one large melon, cut it into quarters and pile the strawberries on top.

To blanch almonds, put them into a small saucepan, cover with water and boil for 2 minutes, then drain them and pop off the skins with your fingers.

225g / 8oz ripe strawberries
caster sugar
4 sprigs of mint

16 blanched almonds
2 baby green-fleshed melons, or 1 larger melon

1. Wash and hull the strawberries then cut them into halves or quarters. Put them in a bowl and sprinkle with a little caster sugar.
2. Roughly tear some mint leaves to release the flavour, and add them to the strawberries, along with the almonds.
3. Cut the baby melons in half or, if you're using one large melon, cut it into quarters. Scoop out and discard the seeds and fill the cavities with the strawberry mixture.

SERVES 4

THREE-PEAR SALAD

Although pawpaws aren't pears, their shape qualifies them for inclusion in this pretty, refreshing salad, and their flavour combines extremely well with avocado and dessert pears. This is a good starter or light lunch dish. Having the fruits perfectly ripe makes all the difference, and it's worth buying them a few days in advance, if necessary, and letting them ripen in a fruit bowl.

1 large ripe dessert pear, preferably Comice
juice of 1 lime
1 large ripe pawpaw

1 large ripe avocado pear
sprigs of fresh chervil and slices of lime to decorate

1. Cut the pear into quarters then peel and core it. Cut it into long thin slices and sprinkle with a little of the lime juice.
2. Peel and quarter the pawpaw, scooping out and discarding the seeds, then cut it in the same way as the pear and sprinkle with lime juice.
3. Prepare the avocado similarly, tossing it in the remaining lime juice.
4. Arrange slices of the three 'pears' on individual plates, decorate with the chervil and lime slices and serve as soon as possible.

SERVES 2 AS A LIGHT MEAL, 4 AS A STARTER

OPPOSITE: *(left) Three-Pear Salad, (top) Melon with Strawberries and Mint, (right) Festive Fruit Salad, page 128*

FESTIVE FRUIT SALAD

Fruit with contrasting and toning colours, textures and flavours makes a quick and easy winter dessert with a festive air. Choose whatever fruits you fancy from what is available.

4 clementines	**1 star fruit**
2 sharon fruit	**1 pomegranate**
12 lychees	**8–12 physalis**

1 Peel the clementines then slice them into rounds and put them into a bowl. Wash the sharon fruit, remove the stems and cut the fruit into eighths or smaller segments; add to the bowl.

2 Peel and stone the lychees; wash the star fruit and cut it into thin slices to reveal the starry shapes. Add to the bowl, along with the lychees.

3 Halve the pomegranate then, holding a half over the bowl, scoop out the scarlet seeds with a pointed teaspoon, discarding any tough membranes. Repeat the process with the other half. Stir the seeds gently into the fruit.

4 Gently pull back the outer dry sepals on each physalis to form 'petals'. Arrange the physalis on top of the fruit salad.

SERVES 4

TARRAGON PEAR WITH CREAM CHEESE

This combination is simple but superb, and makes a good light meal or snack. You can control the fat content by your choice of cheese – full-fat cream cheese, medium-fat curd cheese, or even cottage cheese are all suitable.

2–3 lettuce leaves	**salt and freshly**
1 perfectly ripe pear,	**ground black pepper**
preferably Comice or	**125g / 4oz soft white**
Conference	**cheese**
½ tsp red wine vinegar	**sprig of tarragon**

1 Arrange the lettuce leaves on a serving plate. Cut the pear into quarters, then peel and core it. Cut the quarters into long, thin slices and arrange these on top of the lettuce leaves.

2 Sprinkle the vinegar over the pear, then top with plenty of coarsely ground black pepper and a less generous scattering of salt – preferably the type you can scrunch up with your fingers.

3 Put the cheese on the plate next to the pear slices, then tear some of the lower leaves from the tarragon over the top and decorate with the tender top part of the tarragon sprig.

SERVES 1

APRICOTS WITH RICOTTA AND MINT

This is only worth doing if you can get really ripe, well-flavoured apricots. It makes a lovely light dish, somewhere between a starter, salad and a dessert! I like it as a summery lunch or supper when I'm not feeling very hungry.

3–4 ripe apricots	**a little milk or single**
2–3 tsp clear honey	**cream**
75–125g / 3–4oz	**4–6 fresh mint leaves**
ricotta cheese	

1 Halve, stone and slice the apricots then put them into a bowl with the honey and mix gently.

2 Put the ricotta cheese into another bowl and mix in enough milk or cream to make a soft, creamy consistency. Then spoon it on top of the apricots but do not cover them completely.

3 Tear the mint leaves roughly and scatter on top. Serve as soon as possible.

SERVES 1

FRESH FRUIT PLATTER

Choose fruits that contrast well in colour and texture – figs, kiwi fruit, redcurrants, raspberries, strawberries, apricots, blueberries and cherries all look good. The more people you are making this for, the more varieties of fruit you can use.

175g–225g / 6–8oz fresh fruit per person

sprigs of mint, edible flowers, flaked almonds or crushed pistachios to decorate (optional)

1 Wash and prepare the fruit and cut some in halves or quarters if you like. Figs look especially attractive when quartered.

2 Arrange the fruit on a platter. Decorate, if you wish, with mint sprigs, edible flowers such as borage or nasturtium, or almonds or pistachios.

ORANGE AND KIWI FRUIT SALAD

This is a very fresh-looking and fresh-tasting fruit salad, perfect after a rich main course.

2 kiwi fruit
1 large orange
1 tbls orange blossom honey

½ tsp orange flower water

1 Peel the kiwi fruit then slice them thinly into rounds and put them into a bowl.

2 Holding the orange over the bowl, cut off the peel with a sawing motion, removing all the white pith with the rind. Then cut the segments out from between the membranes and add to the bowl.

3 Add the honey and orange flower water to the fruit and mix gently. Leave in a cool place until ready to serve.

SERVES 1–2

Orange flower water is available from good kitchen shops, Middle Eastern shops and supermarkets, but you can leave it out if you can't get it.

COLD PUDDINGS

*

BANANAS WITH CREAM AND SESAME CRISP

You can vary the richness of this, using just Greek yogurt or, at the other extreme, just cream. If you don't want to go to the trouble of making the sesame crisp – although it couldn't be easier – buy some sesame crisp bars and use them instead.

2 tbls sesame seeds
6 tbls caster sugar
150ml / 5fl oz
 whipping cream
150ml / 5fl oz Greek
 yogurt
4 large bananas

1 First make the sesame crisp: have ready a square of non-stick paper. Put the sesame seeds into a small heavy-based saucepan with the sugar and place over the heat. After a minute or so the sugar will melt and then within a few seconds it will turn golden. At this point, remove it from the stove and pour it in a thin layer over the non-stick paper. Leave on one side to harden.

2 Whip the cream then fold it carefully into the Greek yogurt.

3 Peel and slice the bananas, then put them into one large or four individual bowls. Spoon the yogurt cream on top.

4 Peel the paper off the sesame crisp, then crush it into pieces by banging it with a rolling pin; scatter the pieces on top of the bananas and cream.

SERVES 4

HONEYED PEARS WITH ALMOND HALVA

Almond halva, a delicious Middle Eastern confection, can be bought in large supermarkets, delicatessens or Middle Eastern grocery shops. If you can't get it, you could use good-quality nougat instead. Chopped up and sprinkled over ripe fresh fruit, halva makes a good topping, and turns a simple fruit dish into a more substantial dessert. It works best with delicately flavoured, sweet fruit such as pears or bananas.

4 large ripe pears,
 preferably Comice
juice of ½ lemon
3–4 tbls mild honey,
 clear or thick
75–125g / 3–4oz
 almond halva

1 Cut the pears into quarters then peel and core them. Cut the quarters into long, thin slices, put them into a mixing bowl and toss them in the lemon juice to preserve their colour.

2 Put the honey into a pan, judging the amount according to the sweetness of the pears and your own preference. Heat gently until it is liquid, then pour it over the pears. Stir the pears gently and leave on one side until you are ready to serve them.

3 Chop the halva into small pieces. Transfer the pears to one large serving bowl or four individual ones, top with the halva, then serve.

SERVES 4

OPPOSITE: *(left) Fresh Fruit Platter, page 129, (centre) Orange and Kiwi Fruit Salad, page 129, (right) Bananas with Cream and Sesame Crisp*

131

RASPBERRIES WITH LEMON SYLLABUB

In this recipe, a tangy syllabub is layered with sweet fresh raspberries. It looks good served in tall glasses – wine glasses are ideal – and other fruit could be used instead of the raspberries. Try it with strawberries, substituting orange for the lemon in the syllabub.

200ml / 7fl oz
  whipping cream
grated rind and juice
  of ½ lemon

25–50g / 1–2oz caster
  sugar
225g / 8oz raspberries

1 Put the cream into a bowl with the lemon rind and juice and 25g/1oz caster sugar, then whisk until the mixture forms soft peaks. Taste and add more sugar if necessary, remembering that the raspberries will be slightly sharp.
2 Starting with raspberries, layer the raspberries and the lemon syllabub into two tall glasses. Chill until needed.
SERVES 2

STRAWBERRY FOOL

This is a simple recipe, with the fruit just crushed then folded into a mixture of yogurt and cream. For a lower-fat version, use all yogurt or a larger proportion of yogurt to cream. Other fruits can be used: ripe peaches or apricots, for instance.

225g / 8oz strawberries
25–40g / 1–1½oz
  caster sugar
150ml / 5fl oz
  whipping cream

150ml / 5fl oz plain
  yogurt

1 Wash the strawberries, remove the stems and slice the fruit roughly. Put it into a large bowl and sprinkle with sugar to taste.
2 Whisk the cream until it stands in soft peaks.

3 Add the yogurt to the strawberries, then mash them into the yogurt with a fork, but don't make the mixture smooth.
4 Fold the whipped cream into the yogurt and strawberries. Taste, and gently stir in a little more sugar if necessary.
SERVES 2–3

FRESH PINEAPPLE FOOL

You really need a sweet, well-flavoured pineapple for this recipe – choose a ripe, strongly scented one. It is tempting to make a lower-fat version using half cream and half yogurt, but I don't find that it works as well – yogurt is fairly acidic, whereas the richness of double cream balances the natural sharpness of the pineapple.

1 ripe pineapple
juice of 1 orange
25g / 1oz caster sugar,
  or to taste
2 tbls orange liqueur,
  such as Cointreau or
  Grand Marnier

300ml / ½ pint double
  cream
chopped pistachio
  nuts or fresh mint
  leaves to decorate
  (optional)

1 Peel the pineapple, removing all the tufts and the hard inner core, then chop it fairly finely or purée it in a food processor.
2 Add the orange juice to the pineapple and sprinkle with the sugar and the liqueur.
3 Whip the cream until it forms soft peaks – the acidity of the pineapple will firm it up a bit, so don't make it too stiff. Then fold the pineapple gently into the cream. Taste, and sweeten with a little more sugar if necessary.
4 Spoon the mixture into tall glasses or individual bowls and chill well before serving. Decorate with chopped pistachio nuts or fresh mint leaves, if you like.
SERVES 4

FRUIT AND ICE-CREAM

Good-quality bought ice-cream, mixed with fresh fruit and other extras such as nuts, alcohol, chocolate or coffee, makes an almost instant dessert that is popular with most people. Decent vanilla ice-cream goes with almost any fruit, and good fruit sorbets are also useful. More strongly flavoured ice-creams, such as chocolate or ginger, can be very effective if you pair them with the right fruit. Here are some ideas.

1 VANILLA ICE-CREAM WITH MELON AND GINGER

If you can get ripe, sweet baby melons, serve them cut in half and topped with a scoop of vanilla ice-cream, some chopped preserved ginger and some of its syrup. Or you could use a larger melon cut into pieces.

2 VANILLA ICE-CREAM WITH RUM RAISINS AND HOT CHOCOLATE SAUCE

For each person, put 1 tablespoon of raisins and 1 tablespoon of rum into a small pan and heat gently, then leave on one side to steep. Make the chocolate sauce (see page 140). Let the ice-cream soften at room temperature while you eat your main course then fold the raisins and rum into the ice-cream and pour the chocolate sauce over the top.

3 VANILLA ICE-CREAM WITH BANANAS AND COFFEE

Make some espresso coffee – good-quality instant espresso will do. Slice a banana into a bowl, top with a scoop of vanilla ice-cream then pour the hot coffee over the top. Some whipped cream is good with this, too, if you really want to go to town.

4 VANILLA ICE-CREAM WITH ARMAGNAC PRUNES

Allow about 4 prunes for each serving – they should be the plump, ready-to-eat type. Put them into a shallow dish and sprinkle with 1 tablespoon of Armagnac, then leave them to steep – the longer you can leave them the better. Serve with a scoop of vanilla ice-cream and some toasted flaked almonds, if you like.

5 LEMON SORBET WITH RASPBERRY SAUCE

Make the raspberry sauce (see page 136). Pour a pool of sauce on to each plate and top with some good-quality lemon sorbet.

6 MANGO SORBET WITH EXOTIC FRUITS

Make bought mango sorbet into a festive dessert by serving it in scoops surrounded by pieces of exotic fruit: mango, lychee, pawpaw, sharon fruit, physalis – whatever is available. Passion fruit sorbet is also good served like this.

7 CHOCOLATE ICE-CREAM WITH PEARS, CHERRIES OR ORANGES

Serve scoops of rich chocolate ice-cream with any of these fruits, perhaps tossed with a little liqueur or eau de vie: poire William for pears, kirsch for cherries (they should be juicy dark ones, with the stones removed), Grand Marnier or Cointreau for oranges. Strawberries are also good: marinate these in an orange-flavoured liqueur.

8 COFFEE ICE-CREAM WITH PEARS AND MAPLE SYRUP

Peel and slice a ripe pear for each person; top with scoops of softened coffee ice-cream, drizzle over some maple syrup, and sprinkle with chopped pecan nuts.

9 STRAWBERRY ICE-CREAM WITH PEACHES AND AMARETTI

Skin and slice a large ripe peach for each person; top with a scoop of strawberry ice-cream and some softly whipped cream, then sprinkle over 2–3 crushed amaretti biscuits.

When you buy maple syrup, read the label to make sure it's the real stuff and not 'maple-flavoured syrup'. It's expensive but a little goes a long way and it keeps very well in the fridge.

RHUBARB AND GINGER COMPOTE

Fresh-tasting and succulent, this is good with almond- or orange-flavoured biscuits and some thick yogurt or cream. It can be served either cold or hot.

2 pieces of stem ginger preserved in syrup	*50g / 2oz sugar*
1kg / 2lb rhubarb	*4 tbls ginger syrup from the jar*

1 Finely chop the ginger. Trim the rhubarb and remove any stringy bits then cut it into 2.5 cm/ 1 inch lengths. Wash these, then put them into a pan with the sugar, ginger syrup and chopped ginger, reserving some ginger for decoration.

2 Cover and leave to cook very gently for 2–3 minutes. Stir gently, then cook for a further 2–3 minutes, until the rhubarb is tender. Decorate with the reserved chopped ginger before serving.
SERVES 4

FRESH FRUIT MUESLI

We usually think of muesli as a cereal-based breakfast dish, but the original version was served for supper and was prepared mostly of fruit, usually grated apple. Made like this, with the addition of honey, nuts and plain yogurt, muesli makes a good pudding or, as I sometimes like to eat it, a complete lunch or supper dish.

2 tbls raisins	*1 large sweet eating apple or pear*
150ml / 5fl oz plain yogurt	*2 tbls toasted flaked almonds or hazelnuts*
1–1 ½ tbls clear honey	*single cream (optional)*
1 tbls rolled oats	

1 Put the raisins into a small bowl, cover with a little boiling water and leave to plump up.

2 Put the yogurt into a bowl and add 1 tablespoon of the honey and the oats.

3 Wash the apple or pear then grate it quite coarsely into the bowl on top of the yogurt. Drain the raisins and add them to the bowl, then gently stir everything together.

4 Top with the almonds or hazelnuts. You can drizzle a little more honey over the top if you want to make it sweeter, and serve with some single cream for a richer version.
SERVES 1

MARINATED NECTARINES AND RASPBERRIES

A quick but good summer dessert. Unless the fruit is particularly sweet, I think it needs a little help – you could use either sugar or a mild, clear honey, whichever you prefer.

2 ripe nectarines	*1–2 tbls kirsch, eau de framboise or eau de vie (optional)*
450g / 1lb fresh raspberries	
25–50g / 1–2oz sugar, or a little clear honey	

1 Halve, stone and slice the nectarines then put them into a bowl. Wash the raspberries gently, then add them to the bowl.

2 Add sugar or honey to taste, and the alcohol, if you're using this. Stir gently, then leave to marinate for 15–30 minutes.
SERVES 2–3

OPPOSITE: *Rhubarb and Ginger Compote*

135

PEACHES IN WINE

Ideally this should be made in advance to give the flavours time to develop, so prepare it before you start making the rest of the meal. Light biscuits and some thick creamy yogurt, lightly whipped cream or good-quality vanilla ice-cream go well with it.

4–6 large ripe peaches   **sugar**
300ml / ½ pint sweet
  white wine

1. Put the peaches into a bowl, cover them with boiling water for 2 minutes, until the skins loosen, then slip off the skins with a sharp knife.
2. Halve, stone and thinly slice the peaches. Put them into a bowl – a pretty glass one looks good – and pour over the wine.
3. Sweeten the mixture with a little sugar to taste, then cover the bowl and chill for as long as possible before serving.
SERVES 4

STRAWBERRIES IN RASPBERRY SAUCE

This is an ideal pudding to make in the early summer, when strawberries are at their best. You can use frozen raspberries for the sauce if fresh ones aren't available.

450g / 1lb raspberries   **450g / 1lb strawberries**
2 tbls caster sugar, or
  to taste

1. Purée the raspberries in a food processor then pass them through a nylon sieve to remove the seeds. Stir in the sugar.
2. Wash and hull the strawberries, then slice them. Mix the strawberries with the raspberry sauce; taste, and add more sugar if necessary.
SERVES 4

Strawberries in raspberry sauce are good on their own or with a dollop of thick Greek-style yogurt or crème fraîche and some crisp, delicate biscuits.

FRUITS IN LIQUEUR OR BRANDY

Marinating ripe fresh fruits in liqueur, brandy or eau de vie is a great way to turn them into a dessert. The longer you leave them to soak the better; if you prepare them before you start making the rest of the meal the flavours will have a chance to emerge. Choose really ripe, sweet fruit.

TRY THE FOLLOWING COMBINATIONS:
Pineapple (make sure it is really ripe) or black cherries with kirsch
Satsumas, clementines or tangerines, peeled and sliced into thin rings, with an orange liqueur such as Grand Marnier
Strawberries with orange liqueur
Peaches with brandy
Plums with Amaretto (the plums must be very sweet and ripe)
Pear (my favourite) preferably a perfectly ripe Comice, peeled, sliced and sprinkled with poire William liqueur

1. Peel, trim, core and slice the fruit as necessary – the smaller the pieces, the more they'll absorb the flavours.
2. Put the fruit into a bowl, sweeten with a little sugar to taste and pour over a few tablespoons of your chosen alcohol.
3. You can add extras just before serving, such as a sprinkling of pistachio nuts, flaked almonds or some flakes of plain chocolate. Serve accompanied by yogurt, cream and/or biscuits, if you like.

GRAPES IN BEAUMES DE VENISE

This is good served in large wine glasses – so you can drink the last drops of delicious juice! It doesn't really need any accompaniment, although you could consider a delicate, almondy biscuit to go with it.

225–350g / 8–12oz
  sweet grapes, white
  or a mixture of white,
  red and black

about 150ml / 5fl oz
  Beaumes de Venise

☐1 Wash and halve the grapes and remove the pips. Put the grapes into two glasses or a glass serving bowl.
☐2 Pour the Beaumes de Venise over the grapes and leave until you are ready to serve – but don't chill them as this dulls the flavour.
SERVES 2

MELON, GINGER AND KIWI COMPOTE

This is a very good way of improving the flavour of a melon that isn't as good as it might be. Ginger preserve is used for flavouring and sweetening – or you could use chopped preserved ginger from a jar, with some of the syrup.

1 medium-sized melon   **4 kiwi fruit**
4 tbls ginger preserve

☐1 Halve the melon and remove the seeds, then chop the flesh into pieces and put them into a bowl with the ginger preserve.
☐2 Peel the kiwi fruit and cut them into fairly thin slices; add these to the bowl. Stir, then leave until you are ready to serve the pudding – the longer you can leave it, the more the flavours will develop.
SERVES 4

SATSUMAS IN CARAMEL SAUCE

This is a quick and easy way of dressing up satsumas for an elegant dessert. You can, of course, use other members of the satsuma family, such as tangerines or clementines – if they are small you'll need more than four. Very small ones look pretty peeled and served whole on top of the sauce.

175g / 6oz caster sugar   **4 large satsumas**

☐1 Put half the sugar into a small saucepan and heat gently until it melts and becomes caramel coloured – this will take several minutes.
☐2 Standing well back and covering your hand with a cloth, pour in 2 tablespoons of water; the mixture will erupt and turn lumpy.
☐3 Add the remaining sugar and continue to cook over a gentle heat until the sauce has become smooth again.
☐4 Leave the sauce on one side to cool slightly while you peel the satsumas and slice them into thin rounds, if they are large. Then pour the sauce on to four plates, top with the satsumas, and serve.
SERVES 4

HOT PUDDINGS
—— ✳ ——

HOT HONEY PEACHES WITH AMARETTI

This is a good way of cheering up peaches – or indeed other fruits, such as apricots or pears – that are not as sweet and juicy as they might be. They are good with some thick Greek yogurt.

1–2 peaches   **2–3 amaretti biscuits**
2–3 tsp mild honey,
  clear or thick

1 Slice the peaches finely, skinning them first if you prefer, then put them into a small pan, add honey to taste and heat gently.

2 Let the peach slices cook over a low heat for a few more minutes until they are sweet and tender, then serve them straight away with the amaretti biscuits: either leave them whole or crush them and sprinkle them over the peaches.
SERVES 1

BUTTERED APPLES

Mellow eating apples such as Cox's or really tasty Golden Delicious, if you can get them, work best in this recipe – and sweet, ripe pears are also good. It's best served hot, with thick creamy Greek yogurt and perhaps an almond- or orange-flavoured biscuit or shortbread.

450g / 1lb eating   **2 tsp sugar**
  apples   **50g / 2oz sultanas**
15g / ½oz butter

1 Peel and quarter the apples, remove the cores, then cut each quarter into thin slices.

2 Melt the butter in a saucepan and add the apples, sugar and sultanas. Stir, then cook, uncovered, over a gentle heat for about 3–4 minutes, stirring gently from time to time, until the apples have heated through and softened. Serve at once.
SERVES 2

QUICK BLUEBERRY CRUMBLE

A crumble is the most popular of puddings and also one of the quickest to prepare. To speed up the cooking, this one is grilled instead of baked, producing a really good crisp topping. You can use many other types of fruit instead of blueberries. Choose soft fruit that doesn't need pre-cooking.

225g / 8oz blueberries   **125g / 4oz butter**
150g / 5oz plain flour   **15g / ½oz flaked**
125g / 4oz caster sugar   **almonds**

1 Wash the blueberries then put them into a shallow heatproof dish. Heat the grill to medium.

2 To make the crumble, put the flour and sugar into a bowl and rub in the butter with your fingertips. Or whizz all these ingredients together in a food processor fitted with a plastic blade.

3 Arrange the crumble evenly on top of the blueberries and grill for 10–15 minutes or until the crumble is brown and the blueberries bubbling. If the crumble seems to be browning too quickly, cover the dish with foil. Scatter the almonds over the crumble 2–3 minutes before it is ready, removing the foil, if you are using it, so that they brown.
SERVES 2–3

OPPOSITE: *(top) Buttered Apples, (bottom) Quick Blueberry Crumble*

BANANAS OR PEARS WITH HOT CHOCOLATE SAUCE

Chocolate sauce is quick to make and turns bananas or pears into a hot pudding when you want something simple and easy but a bit special.

The better the chocolate, the better the sauce... one with at least 50 percent cocoa solids is best (read the packet) though you don't want too bitter a chocolate for this recipe.

100g / 3½ oz plain chocolate	a few flaked almonds whipped cream (optional)
15g / ½ oz unsalted butter	
4 medium bananas or sweet ripe pears	

1 First make the chocolate sauce: break up the chocolate and put it into a small saucepan with the butter and 75ml/3fl oz of water. Heat gently until the chocolate has melted.

2 Peel and slice the bananas, or peel, core and slice the pears. Arrange in four individual dishes.

3 Give the chocolate sauce a stir then pour it over the fruit just before you want to serve it. Top with a few flaked almonds, and a little whipped cream if you are using this.

SERVES 4

FLAMBEED FRUIT

This is good made with tropical fruits: bananas and pineapple work particularly well. It's quite dramatic when the flames go up, so stand well back.

1 small ripe pineapple	juice of 1 orange
2 large bananas	4 tbls dark rum
25g / 1oz unsalted butter	toasted flaked coconut or toasted flaked almonds (optional)
25g / 1oz brown sugar	

1 Peel the pineapple, removing the tufts and hard core, then cut it into medium-sized chunks. Peel and slice the bananas.

2 Melt the butter and sugar in a saucepan then add the fruit and orange juice. Cook, stirring, for 3–4 minutes, until the fruit is heated through.

3 Put the rum into a small saucepan or metal ladle and warm it over the gas flame or hot plate. When it is tepid, set it alight with a match, standing well back and averting your face. Tip it into the fruit and let it burn, then serve immediately, sprinkled with the flaked coconut or almonds.
SERVES 4

INDIVIDUAL BANANA AND ALMOND CRUMBLES

4 large bananas	50g / 2oz light brown sugar
125g / 4oz plain flour	
50g / 2oz ground almonds	25g / 1oz flaked almonds
25g / 1oz softened butter	

1 Heat the grill to medium. Peel the bananas and slice each one fairly thinly into a ramekin dish.

2 Sift the flour into a bowl. Add the ground almonds, butter and sugar and mix them to a crumbly consistency with a fork. Then mix in the flaked almonds.

3 Spoon the crumble evenly on top of the bananas then grill for 10–15 minutes, until the topping is crisp and golden brown and the bananas are heated through. If the crumble is getting too brown before the bananas are hot, cover with some foil.
SERVES 4

ORANGE ZABAGLIONE WITH STRAWBERRIES

You can whizz this luxurious pudding up in no time at all with an electric hand whisk; without one it takes a little longer. Sponge fingers or delicate thin almond biscuits go well with it.

175–225g / 6–8oz strawberries	1 tbls orange liqueur, such as Cointreau
3 tbls caster sugar	shreds of orange rind to decorate
2 egg yolks	
grated rind of ½ orange	

1. Set a heatproof bowl over a pan of water and heat until the water is steaming. Make sure the bowl is not touching the water in the pan.
2. Wash and hull the strawberries then halve or slice them. Divide them between two bowls, sprinkle with 1 tablespoon of the caster sugar and leave on one side.
3. Put the egg yolks into the bowl and add the remaining sugar and the grated orange rind. Keeping the bowl over the pan of steaming water, whisk until pale and thick: about 5 minutes with an electric whisk, 10–15 minutes by hand.
4. Stir in the orange liqueur, then spoon the zabaglione over the strawberries, decorate with a few strands of orange rind, and serve at once.
SERVES 2

BANANA FRITTERS WITH LIME

oil for deep-frying	3 bananas
125g / 4oz plain flour	caster sugar
1 tbls melted butter	1 lime, sliced
1 egg white	crème fraîche

1. Set the oven to 150°C/300°F/Gas Mark 2. Heat some oil for deep-frying in a saucepan.
2. Next make the batter: sift the flour into a bowl, make a well in the centre and add the butter and 150ml/5fl oz of water. Mix until smooth. Whisk the egg white until it is standing in stiff peaks, then fold it into the batter.
3. Peel the bananas and cut them into chunks. Dip them into the batter, drain off the excess and fry in the hot oil, a few at a time, for 2–3 minutes, turning them over half way through.
4. Drain the fritters on kitchen paper and keep them warm in the oven while you fry the rest. As soon as they are all done, serve the fritters sprinkled with caster sugar and decorated with slices of lime. Serve the crème fraîche separately in a small bowl.
SERVES 4

PLUMS WITH CINNAMON CRUNCH

This quick, unconventional topping goes well with many types of cooked fresh fruit.

900g / 2lb red plums	125g / 4oz porridge oats
175g / 6oz demerara sugar	1 tsp cinnamon
40g / 1½oz butter	pinch of ground cloves

1. Halve and stone the plums, then cut them into chunky slices. Put them into a saucepan with 2 tablespoons of water and two thirds of the sugar and cook gently until the sugar has melted and the plums are just tender.
2. Preheat the grill. Melt the butter in a separate pan, then stir in the oats and the remaining sugar. Mix well, then spread the mixture on a grill pan or baking sheet and grill for about 10 minutes, stirring often, until the mixture is brown and crisp. Stir in the cinnamon and cloves.
3. Reheat the plums, then transfer them to a pie dish that will fit under your grill, spread the oat mixture on top, and keep warm under the grill until you are ready to serve.
SERVES 4

INDEX